102 Fascinating Bible Studies

ON THE NEW TESTAMENT

Books by Dr. William H. Marty

102 Fascinating Bible Studies on the New Testament

The Jesus Story

*The Quick-Start Guide to the Whole Bible**

The Whole Bible Story

The World of Jesus

*with Dr. Boyd Seevers

102 Fascinating Bible Studies

ON THE NEW TESTAMENT

Dr. William H. Marty

a division of Baker Publishing Group
Minneapolis, Minnesota

Published by Bethany House Publishers
11400 Hampshire Avenue South
Bloomington, Minnesota 55438
www.bethanyhouse.com

Bethany House Publishers is a division of
Baker Publishing Group, Grand Rapids, Michigan

Printed in the United States of America

Library of Congress Cataloging-in-Publication Data
Names: Marty, William Henry, author.
Title: 102 fascinating Bible studies on the New Testament / William H. Marty.
Other titles: One hundred two fascinating Bible studies on the New Testament | One hundred and two fascinating Bible studies on the New Testament
Description: Minneapolis : Bethany House, a division of Baker Publishing Group, 2019. | Identifiers: LCCN 2018039189| ISBN 9780764232435 (trade paper) | ISBN 9781493417186 (e-book)
Subjects: LCSH: Bible. New Testament—Textbooks.
Classification: LCC BS2535.3 .M37 2019 | DDC 225.6/1—dc23
LC record available at https://lccn.loc.gov/2018039189

Cover design by LOOK Design Studio

19 20 21 22 23 24 25   7 6 5 4 3 2 1

In keeping with biblical principles of creation stewardship, Baker Publishing Group advocates the responsible use of our natural resources. As a member of the Green Press Initiative, our company uses recycled paper when possible. The text paper of this book is composed in part of post-consumer waste.

This book is dedicated
to the people who will use it.
It is my hope that it will
help you to better know the Word of God
and the God of the Word.

Contents

Paul's Epistles

General Epistles

Revelation

Doctrine

Introduction

I had the unique privilege of teaching Old and New Testament Survey to four hundred freshmen for thirty-seven years. It was an exciting experience. They were eager to learn, and keenly attentive in class, at least at the beginning of each semester. Of course, since they were at Moody Bible Institute, they expected their Bible teachers to answer all their questions about the Bible, including some that angels never imagined. I soon learned that I would never get through survey if I didn't control their questions, so I had to be somewhat of a killjoy and explain to them that I couldn't answer all their questions. I assured them that in their four years at Moody they would have multiple opportunities to get answers to their questions. I also confessed that I didn't know all of the answers, which was somewhat shocking to some students. But I assured them that my colleagues knew more than I did about certain subjects and would be able to answer their questions.

I'm sorry, but I have to be a killjoy again. This book will answer a lot of your questions, but not all of them. That's the bad news. The good news is that the editor gave me the liberty to pick the topics. When he told me that, I thought he must be kidding. Did he know what he was doing giving a retired Bible teacher that kind of freedom? He was serious, so most of the studies are on topics about which I think I am capable of making a few intelligent comments. But not all. I chose some topics that I had not previously studied but have had questions about. Some are a bit difficult and even controversial. I have tried to avoid tipping my hand on the ones that are controversial, but it is impossible to be completely unbiased. So if you disagree with me on a conclusion, that's okay. I'm not inspired; the Bible is. I realize I may be wrong, and people who disagree are not heretics. Some may have a different interpretation of certain passages. It is possible to agree to disagree if those passages are not foundational to orthodox Christian doctrine.

What's in this book? A lot of studies on topics from the New Testament. At one point, I told the editor I felt like I was writing a Bible dictionary, but I was the only contributor. He was really encouraging. He said that he felt the same way as an editor. How are the topics organized? I tried to balance the studies between the life of Christ (the four Gospels), the book of Acts, Paul's epistles, the general epistles, several studies on the book of Revelation, and doctrine. Because this isn't a story, the order in which you do the studies doesn't matter. You can start with the last study in the book and then go to the next one that captures your interest.

Who should use this book? It is intended for individuals or small groups, for pastors or people in the pew, for Bible teachers or students, for mature believers or new Christians. You don't even have to be a Christian to use this book. You may have serious doubts about Christianity because of what you believe the Bible says or what others have told you the Bible says on certain subjects. You may find one or more of those subjects in the book, and you may be surprised by what the Bible actually says.

What should you do with this book? Don't read it like a novel. It doesn't have a plot and story line. There are "102 Fascinating Bible Studies" in it. Why 102? I don't know. That's how many I was asked to write. The format for each study is basically the same. I make a few comments about the topic that includes some of the significant biblical references. The comments are followed by a memory verse on the topic. The questions are the main part of the study. Don't do what my wife and others have attempted, and that's to answer the questions without reading the passage. If you do, you will tell me what my wife did: "I don't understand!" I then asked her, "Did you read the passage?" The usual answer was, "No!" "Well, no wonder you don't understand the question!" My wife was actually a huge help in writing this book. But please read the passage before attempting to answer or discuss the questions. If you don't like my questions or want to add additional ones, you can make up your own.

The goal for this book is what I have been devoted to most of my adult life. After college, four years in the army, and one tour in Vietnam, I decided I wanted to do something else, so I went to seminary. Seminary was like landing on a different planet. The men and women who were my teachers not only cared for me, but they loved God and his Word. Their passion for the Word of God ignited the same passion in me, so after a whole lot of schooling I began ministry and found my place in God's kingdom teaching the Bible to young men and women and trying to ignite in them a love for God and his Word.

My wife thinks I was the right person to write this book. She often tells me that because I didn't grow up in the church, I don't think in the typical evangelical/orthodox Christian box. She said that growing up in the church she was not allowed to ask some of the questions I do. This book will not answer all of your questions, but hopefully it will give you insight and a fresh perspective on some of the perplexing passages in the New Testament. I hope the studies challenge you, make you think, but most of all help you to become more like Christ. In the study on Paul's prayers, I have been convicted to include his prayer for the Ephesians in my prayers for others. "I keep asking that the God of our Lord Jesus Christ, the glorious Father, may give you the Spirit of wisdom and revelation, so that you may know him better" (Ephesians 1:17). And that's my prayer for you!

PART 1

The Life of Christ

Genealogies of Jesus

Because of the advances in DNA testing, there has been a surge of interest in tracing one's ancestry. Though they didn't have DNA testing at the time of Christ, genealogies were extremely important in Judaism. They were essential for establishing inheritance rights and tracing the messianic line.

Only Matthew and Luke give Jesus' ancestry, and though the genealogies are similar they are not identical. Plus, they are not complete, only representative.

Matthew presents Jesus as Israel's messianic king, who had come in fulfillment of God's kingdom promises. No one, however, could claim they were Israel's long-awaited king unless they were a descendant of David, to whom God had promised that one of his descendants would rule over an eternal kingdom (2 Samuel 7:16). Matthew then begins his Gospel by identifying Jesus as the Messiah, a son of David, and a son of Abraham (1:1). By tracing his ancestry to David, Matthew establishes Jesus' legal right to the throne of David. But he also wants to show that Jesus is the fulfillment of the universal promise of the Abrahamic Covenant (Genesis 12:1–3).

Luke's concern is to show that Jesus is a universal Savior. He traces Jesus' ancestry from Joseph to Adam (3:38), and puts the genealogy between Jesus' baptism and temptation (3:21–4:13). By placing the genealogy between Jesus' baptism and temptation Luke contrasts Jesus' victory over sin and Satan as the second Adam with the failure of the first Adam (cf. Luke 3:21–22 and Luke 4:1–3). Because he was created, Adam is called "the son of God" (3:38). God calls Jesus his "beloved Son" at his baptism (3:22 ESV), and in the temptation account, Satan says, "If you are the Son of God . . ." (4:3).

Study Questions

1. Matthew 1:16. Why do you think Matthew identifies Joseph as the husband of Mary rather than the father of Jesus?

2. Matthew 1:3, 5, and 6. In addition to Mary, Matthew lists four women in Jesus' genealogy.
   a) Who are they and what do we know about them from the Old Testament?
   b) What is the significance of including these women in Jesus' genealogy?

3. Genesis 12:1–3. What are the three promises God made to Abraham? How did God fulfill the promise to bless "all people"? Why is this important if we are not Jewish?

4. Matthew 28:16–20. Though Jesus is identified in the genealogy as Israel's Messiah-King, how does the Gospel of Matthew end? Why is this important?

5. Luke 3:23. Like Matthew, Luke makes it clear that Joseph is not Jesus' biological father. Luke's intent is to raise the question, "If Joseph is not Jesus' father, who is?" How does Luke answer that question in 3:38?

6. Luke 3:38. Not only is the order of Jesus' genealogy in the reverse order than the names in Matthew, but Luke does not stop with David and Abraham. How far back does Luke trace Jesus' ancestry? And as mentioned in the commentary, the genealogy comes before the temptation account. Why?

7. Matthew 1:11–13. Who is identified in the genealogy?
   a) What happened to Jehoiachin, king of Judah, because of his wickedness (see Jeremiah 22:24–27)? The "signet ring" was a symbol of royal lineage. This means that the royal line was cut off, and messianic hopes ended with the Babylonian exile.

b) Haggai 2:23. What did God do to reinstate the messianic line?

c) What does this reveal about the grace of God and his promises?

8. What do the genealogies confirm about God's providential control of history? How does this give you assurance about the course of your life?

Memory Verse: Matthew 1:1

2

Birth of Jesus

The Gospels give two complementary accounts of Jesus' birth. Matthew records the birth of Jesus from the perspective of Joseph, Jesus' father, and Luke gives Mary's perspective.

Jesus' birth was a miracle. Before they were married, Joseph discovered his fiancée was pregnant. Joseph was honorable and did not want to disgrace Mary so he planned to divorce (betrothal was as binding as marriage) her secretly. However, the angel Gabriel appeared to him in a dream, saying, "Do not be afraid to take Mary as your wife. For the child within her was conceived by the Holy Spirit" (Matthew 1:20 NLT). Joseph married his fiancée as Gabriel had commanded but did not have sexual relations with her until after the birth of their son (Matthew 1:24–25).

After his announcement to Joseph, Gabriel appeared to Mary and informed her that she would give birth to a son, and she was to name him Jesus. Confused, Mary asked, "But how can this happen? I am a virgin" (Luke 1:34 NLT). Gabriel did not offer Mary a scientific explanation but said she would conceive by the Holy Spirit and the power of the Most High would overshadow her (Luke 1:35). As proof that nothing is impossible with God, Gabriel informed Mary that her cousin Elizabeth had conceived in her old age (Luke 1:36). Mary responded with humility and obedience to the startling revelation. She said, "I am the Lord's servant. May everything you have said about me come true" (Luke 1:38, NLT).

Though Joseph and Mary lived in Nazareth in the northern province of Israel, Jesus was born in Bethlehem, the home of David, in Judea during the rule of Caesar Augustus. Joseph went to Bethlehem, his hometown, to register for a census when Quirinius was governor of Syria (Luke 2:1–4). Because they couldn't find lodging, Jesus was born in a manger, a feeding trough for animals (Luke 2:6–7).

Study Questions

1. Luke 1:35. Why do you think the virgin conception and birth of Jesus is important for the following:
   a. The fulfillment of prophecy (see Isaiah 7:14)
   b. The humanity of Christ
   c. The deity of Christ
   d. That Jesus did not inherit Adam's sin nature
   e. Our salvation, which is also a supernatural work of God (see John 3:5–8; Titus 3:7)
2. How did God work supernaturally and providentially in the birth of Jesus? Can you recall an event or events from your life in which God worked providentially?
3. Matthew 1:21. What was Jesus' primary mission? How important was the virgin birth for Jesus' mission as Savior?
4. Matthew 1:24. How difficult do you think it was for Joseph to respond to Gabriel's revelation that his fiancée would conceive a child by the Holy Spirit? Can you think of a past difficult situation in which you had to respond solely by faith? How does Joseph's response encourage you in your daily walk with Christ?
5. Luke 1:42. Why did Elizabeth bless Mary? Do you know a person you can honor (bless) because of their obedience to the Lord?

Memory Verse: Galatians 4:4–5

3

Infancy and Childhood of Jesus

The Gospel writers do not provide extended information about Jesus' infancy and childhood. Instead, Matthew focuses on events that fulfilled prophecy, while Luke focuses on Jesus' humanity. Neither Mark nor John give any information about Jesus' birth or childhood.

As faithful Jews, Joseph and Mary dedicated Jesus in the temple according to the law of Moses. At the dedication, Simeon, a righteous man, and Anna, a prophetess, prophesied about the child Jesus and praised God (Luke 2:21–38). Luke's summary of Jesus' growth indicates that it was normal, "And the child grew and became strong; he was filled with wisdom, and the grace of God was on him" (Luke 2:40).

Miracle stories such as Jesus making live pigeons from clay are from apocryphal (false) gospels, not the canonical Gospels. The only biblical account of Jesus' childhood comes from Luke, who records Jesus' parents taking him to Jerusalem for Passover when he was twelve (Luke 2:41–49). When they began the journey back to Nazareth, they inadvertently left Jesus behind, thinking he was with an extended family member. They returned to Jerusalem to search for Jesus and found him discussing the Law with the elders in the temple. When they reprimanded their son for not staying with them, Jesus responded, "Didn't you know I had to be in my Father's house?" (Luke 2:49). This statement is important because it reveals that at an early age Jesus was aware of his unique Father-Son relationship.

We know that Jesus could read and write. John records Jesus writing in the sand when the religious leaders brought to Jesus a woman caught in adultery (John 8:1–11, *This passage is not included in some of the earliest manuscripts.*). Jesus read from the scroll of Isaiah when he spoke in the synagogue at Nazareth (Luke 4:16–20). Jesus would have been educated in the synagogue and at home. He was trilingual, speaking Aramaic, Greek, and Hebrew.

Jesus' parents were not wealthy. Joseph was a carpenter, which meant he worked with wood, stone, or even metal (Mark 6:3). Jesus also had brothers and sisters (Mark 6:3), though Roman Catholic scholars claim these are cousins in order to preserve the perpetual virginity of Mary.

Study Questions

1. Luke 2:39–40. Why do you think the biblical writers do not give us more information about Jesus' childhood? What else would you like to know about Jesus and why?
2. Luke 4:16–20. Do you think Jesus had to study the Old Testament or did he know it because he was the Son of God? Why or why not?
3. Luke 2:41–49. How do you think Jesus became aware that God was his Father?
4. Mark 6:3. Why do you think God chose common people like Joseph and Mary to become the parents of the Son of God? What does this suggest about the kind of people that the Lord uses?
5. Luke 2:21–38. Do you think it was important for Joseph and Mary to dedicate Jesus in the temple as required by the law of Moses? Is baby dedication important today? Why or why not?
6. Matthew 13:53–58. Why do people today have questions about Jesus Christ?

7. Galatians 4:4. What is the implication about the person of Christ?

8. Mark 3:35. Who does Jesus say is his true family? What does this mean to you?

Memory Verse: Luke 2:39–40

4

John the Baptist

When I was in college we were required to have a Christian service assignment. I chose to serve on an evangelistic team to Jewish people led by Moishe Rosen. Moishe was a modern-day John the Baptist. He took our team to MacArthur Park in Los Angeles on Sunday afternoon where Jewish people gathered to relax. We would set up in a strategic location and preach in the open air to anyone who would listen. Sometimes our audience was mostly pigeons. Most Jewish people would listen politely, but some would become argumentative and even abusive. Moishe was fearless. People would scream at him, spit at him, and throw things. Moishe was a big man, weighing over two hundred pounds. One time a small elderly man attacked him with a cane. It was both humorous and scary. This little man was swinging wildly with his cane at this giant of a man, and Moishe was backpedaling across the park. If I remember correctly, the elderly man got tired and gave up. As a young college student I thought for sure Moishe would get us killed. Moishe later founded Jews for Jesus and continued his bold and aggressive strategy of evangelism.

Like Moishe, John the Baptist was a street preacher. He didn't preach in the synagogue or the temple but in the wilderness (Mark 1:4). His message was blunt. He said, "Repent, for the kingdom of heaven has come near" (Matthew 3:2). He didn't wear designer clothes like other religious leaders. He wore a coarse garment of camel's hair with a leather belt and ate locusts and wild honey (Mark 1:6). He was the last of the Old Testament prophets but had the most important mission of all—to prepare the way for the coming of the Messiah (Mark 1:2–8).

Study Questions

1. Luke 1:5–25
    a. Who were the parents of John the Baptist? How does Luke describe their circumstances?
    b. What happened to reverse their circumstances?
    c. Can you recall a situation in your life when your circumstances were unexpectedly changed for the better? Do you believe that God was at work? Why or why not?

2. Matthew 3:1–12
    a. Why do you think John lived and ministered in the wilderness (desert)? If John were alive today where do you think he would preach?
    b. What was John's warning to the Pharisees and Sadducees? What would his warning be to America?
    c. With what did John say the Messiah (Jesus) would baptize people? In the context of verse 12, what is the most likely meaning of "fire"?

3. Luke 3:7–20
    a. What three groups of people are identified, and what was John's message to each of these groups?
    b. Identify three contemporary groups of people and explain what your message would be to each of these groups.

4. Matthew 11:11
    a. Why did Jesus say John was greater than anyone else? (Don't peek at the answer.)

        It was because John had the privilege and responsibility of pointing people directly to Jesus Christ. All of the other prophets could only prophesy about the future coming of the Messiah.

b. Why did Jesus then say those who are "least" in the kingdom of God are greater than John? (Don't peek.)

Because those who came after John were able to know the complete story of Jesus (his life, death, and resurrection), trust him as Savior, and enter into the kingdom.

c. Are you greater than John? Why?

Memory Verse: John 1:29–31

5

Baptism of Jesus

The baptism of Jesus is recorded in the Synoptic Gospels (Mathew, Mark, and Luke). Mark records that when Jesus was baptized by John in the Jordan River, the heavens were torn open, the Holy Spirit descended on Jesus like a dove, and God spoke from heaven (1:9–11). Luke places the baptism account immediately before the genealogy (3:21–22), not the temptation as in Matthew and Mark. He adds that Jesus was praying when he was baptized and that the Holy Spirit descended on Jesus in bodily form.

Matthew's account is the longest (3:13–17). He reveals that when Jesus approached John for baptism, the prophet questioned him. He knew that Jesus was sinless and did not need forgiveness. Jesus' answer is puzzling. He said he needed baptism "to fulfill all righteousness" (v. 15). Matthew also gives a different perspective on the voice from heaven. Instead of speaking directly to Jesus, Matthew states that God spoke to those present, publicly declaring, "This is my Son, whom I love; with him I am well pleased" (v. 17).

Study Questions

1. Luke 3:22; Acts 10:38; Luke 4:14–15. When was Jesus filled with the Spirit? What is the significance of this for Jesus' ministry?

2. Mark 1:1–11. How did Jesus' baptism, especially the visible descent of the Spirit and God's voice from heaven, validate the ministry of John the Baptist?

3. Luke 3:21–22; Acts 2:38–41; 8:12; 9:17–18; 10:46–48. How is Jesus' baptism a model for believers' baptism? How is it different?

4. Matthew 3:13–15; Isaiah 53:4–6; 2 Corinthians 5:21. Though John was right when he questioned Jesus about the necessity of baptism, why do you think Jesus insisted on baptism? What did Jesus mean when he said it was necessary "to fulfill all righteousness"? Why do you think it is important for believers to be baptized today?

5. Luke 3:22. Why do you think Luke emphasized that the Spirit descended on Jesus in a visible body? What are the implications of this for the Holy Spirit? Is the Spirit a power or a person?

6. Mark 1:11; Luke 3:22; Psalm 2:7. Mark and Luke record that God spoke directly to Jesus. Why do you think God assured Jesus that he was his beloved Son? Believers are called children of God but not sons of God (1 John 3:1). How is Jesus God's unique Son?

7. John 1:32–34. Though John does not record the actual baptism of Jesus, what does he say convinced him that Jesus was "the Chosen One of God" (NLT) or "the Son of God" (ESV)? What convinced you that Jesus was the Son of God?

8. Mark 1:11; 9:1–8; John 12:27–29. God spoke three times during the earthly life of Jesus. The first two were at his baptism and the transfiguration. What was the third time? Why do you think God spoke on these three occasions?

9. Matthew 3:16–17; 1 Samuel 10:1; 16:13. In the Old Testament, prophets anointed kings with oil to identify them as chosen by God. Matthew emphasizes that Jesus came as Israel's messianic king. (He was a descendant of David.) How does Jesus' baptism compare to the anointing of kings? Who anointed Jesus? What is the evidence of his anointing?

10. Matthew 3:13–17. Many have observed that all three persons of the Trinity were present at Jesus' baptism—the Father, the Son, and the Holy Spirit. This was the only occasion during the life of Jesus that all three persons of the Trinity appeared at one time. Why do you think all three persons were present? Why was this important for Jesus? For the witnesses present (the Jewish nation)?

Memory Verse: Matthew 3:16–17

6

Temptations of Jesus

Matthew, Mark, and Luke record the temptations of Jesus. Mark gives the shortest account (1:12–13). He only mentions that Jesus was tempted, and does not describe the three temptations. Matthew (4:1–11) and Luke (4:1–13) are similar but not identical. Each explain that Jesus was tempted three times but give a different order for the second and third temptations. The first in both is the temptation for Jesus to turn stones to bread to satisfy his hunger. In Matthew the second is the temptation to test God by leaping from the temple, and the third is the promise of the kingdoms of the world in exchange for worshiping Satan. The order of the second and third is reversed in Luke's Gospel.

The theological issue raised by the temptations of Jesus is the statement in James 1:13 that "God cannot be tempted." Since Jesus was fully God, how could he have been tempted? Yet the writer to the Hebrews states that Jesus is able to sympathize with us in our humanness because he was tempted in the same way we are yet didn't sin (Hebrews 4:15).

Study Questions

1. Mark 1:12–13. Though his account is short, what does Mark include that is not found in Matthew and Luke? Why?
2. Matthew 4:4, 7, and 10 and Luke 4:4, 8, and 12. Why is it important to know Scripture when resisting temptation?
3. Genesis 3:1–7. What are the similarities between the nature of the temptations of Adam and Eve and Jesus? What are

the similarities between the temptations of Jesus and the temptations we face (1 John 2:15–17)?

4. Matthew 4:5–7. How was this a temptation to test God, and what are some of the ways that we test God?

5. Matthew 4:4, 7, and 10. What Old Testament book is the source of all of the Scripture Jesus quoted in resisting Satan? All of the references are related to Israel's experiences in the wilderness. What is the difference between Jesus' and Israel's response to testing? Why did Matthew make this comparison?

6. James 1:12–15. In the introduction the fact that God cannot be tempted raises a question about temptation and Jesus' deity (that he was fully God). Hebrews 4:14–16 makes it clear that because Jesus was a man he did experience temptation but did not sin. How would you explain the union of two natures, Jesus' deity and humanity, in relation to the temptations? Do you think Jesus' temptations were real? Why or why not?

7. Luke 4:13. The encounter with Satan in the wilderness was not the only time Jesus was tempted. He was tempted when he predicted his death and Peter protested (Matthew 16:23) and when he prayed in the garden of Gethsemane (Mark 14:32–42). Do you think temptation is a lifelong experience? If so, how should we protect ourselves from becoming victims?

8. Luke 4:1. Luke says that when Jesus was tempted he was "full of the Holy Spirit." Matthew states that the Spirit led Jesus into the wilderness (4:1). Mark is the most forceful, writing that the Spirit "drove" Jesus into the wilderness (1:12 ESV). The encounter between Jesus and Satan was clearly not an ambush; it was the will of God. Why do you

think it was necessary for Jesus to show his power over Satan and sin prior to beginning his earthly ministry?

9. Luke 4:1 and Ephesians 5:18. How important was it for Jesus to be filled with the Holy Spirit when tempted? How does the Spirit help us when we are tempted?

Memory Verse: Hebrews 4:15

7

Water to Wine

JESUS' FIRST SIGN MIRACLE

John refers to Jesus' miracles as "signs." A sign points to the meaning of the event rather than its miraculous aspect. John records seven of Jesus' "sign miracles" in the main body of his Gospel. The first is turning water to wine at a wedding in Cana of Galilee (2:1–12).

Many believe that because Jesus' first miracle was at a wedding, this was his endorsement of marriage. Jesus was a faithful Jew, and Jews valued marriage because it was established by God. It is unlikely, however, that Jesus needed to show his approval of marriage. Some have compared the miracle to Moses' turning water to blood when he inflicted plagues on the Egyptians. This interpretation is also unlikely because the water to blood was an act of judgment; Jesus' turning water to wine was a blessing.

The meaning of this sign miracle comes from the Old Testament. To describe God's kingdom, the prophets used the imagery of a banquet with a super abundant supply of wine, which the Jews associated with divine favor. Amos describes the messianic kingdom as wine dripping from the mountains and flowing from the hills (Amos 9:13–15; cf. Isaiah 25:6; 55:1).

When they ran out of wine at the wedding, Jesus turned six large jars of water into wine. This would have produced between 120 and 180 gallons of wine (450 to 680 liters). Jesus was not encouraging binge drinking, and the wedding party did not need that much wine. He was symbolizing that with his coming the kingdom had arrived with unlimited blessings of salvation for everyone. John previously declared that Jesus brought an age of unlimited grace:

"Out of his fullness we have all received grace in place of grace already given" (John 1:16).

Study Questions

1. John 2:1–4. Why did Jesus initially refuse his mother's request to help with the problem? The term *woman* isn't harsh or disrespectful, but Jesus used it to remind his mother that she did not have ultimate authority over him.
2. John 2:6. What was the purpose of the water? How do people today attempt to wash away their sins?
3. John 2:8–10; 1:15–18. What is the significance of Jesus' filling the jars with "the best" wine? Can you describe some of the ways that Christ's coming has brought blessings that exceed the Old Testament (law vs. grace)?
4. Isaiah 25:6–8. What are the blessings that Isaiah promises with the coming of the kingdom? How did Jesus fulfill the promise in verse 8?
5. John 2:10. What do you think is meant by the statement "you have saved the best till now"? What are some of the ways your life has changed because you trusted Christ as your Savior?
6. John 2:11; 1:14. What is the "glory" that Jesus revealed in this miracle? One of the themes in John's Gospel is the revelation of God's glory in the life of Jesus. Read Jesus' prayer for himself in John 17:1–5 and consider the following:
   a. What did Jesus mean by "the hour has come"?
   b. How did Jesus bring glory to his Father?
   c. What does verse 5 reveal about the person of Christ before his incarnation (his earthly life in the flesh)?

d. Though we cannot do what Jesus did because he was the Son of God, what are some ways we can bring glory to God?

Memory Verse: John 2:11

8

Beatitudes

MATTHEW 5:1–12

The Sermon on the Mount is the first of five major discourses (sermons) in the Gospel of Matthew. The traditional location for the sermon is in the north on a mountainside overlooking the Sea of Galilee. There is a shorter version in Luke, with a slight variation in location (Luke 6:17–49). Though Jesus had attracted large crowds, he spoke mainly to his disciples (Matthew 5:1).

The sermon is not about how to enter the kingdom of God (salvation). It describes various aspects of the lifestyle for those already in the kingdom. Jesus counters the Pharisees' emphasis on external righteousness; instead he insists on internal righteousness that is from the heart (Matthew 5:20). Paul uses righteousness primarily to describe a person's legal standing before God. Jesus uses it to describe the values and habits of life that are pleasing to God.

The Beatitudes are the introduction to the Sermon on the Mount and give the spiritual values that empower the lifestyle Jesus describes in the sermon (Matthew 5:12–7:29). The term *beatitude* comes from the Latin word for blessing. The Greek term is *makarios*, usually translated "blessed," and refers to a state of contentment knowing that one is approved by God. Though some count nine beatitudes, the most natural numbering is eight with the last one repeated for emphasis (Matthew 5:10–12).

Study Questions

1. Matthew 5:3. Here *poor* is more about recognition of one's spiritual need. In Luke 6:20 it refers to economic poverty. It is true that in the Old Testament "the poor" are generally

more pious, more willing to recognize their need for God's blessing; but it is not physical poverty that makes a person blessed. Poor people can be just as arrogant and ungodly as the rich. How would you describe a person who is "poor in spirit"?

2. Matthew 5:4; 2 Corinthians 1:3–7. We mourn for what we care about. What breaks your heart? How has God comforted you when you have experienced emotional pain?

3. Matthew 5:5; Micah 6:8. What does it mean for you to "walk humbly" with God? "Inherit the earth" is most likely a reference to enjoying the blessings of God's kingdom when he rules over the entire earth.

4. Matthew 5:6; Micah 6:8. To "hunger and thirst for righteousness" could refer to an intense longing to be right with God or have justice for everyone when God establishes his kingdom. What can we do as Christians to correct injustice in the world or in our community in anticipation of God's kingdom?

5. Matthew 5:7; 6:12. Mercy is the withholding of judgment and is the result of forgiveness. We are more inclined to be judgmental than merciful. How can you develop a mind-set of mercy? Can you recall two instances where you extended mercy to someone in the past year?

6. Matthew 5:8. Why is being "pure in heart" a prerequisite for seeing God? What are some of the attitudes that can contaminate our hearts? Is there something you need to do to purify your heart?

7. Matthew 5:9. Peace is the absence of hostility. Though Jesus warned of trouble in the world, he promised us peace in him (John 16:33), and Paul urges us to live at peace with everyone (Romans 12:18). If needed, how can you be a peacemaker in your family or church?

8. Matthew 5:10–12. Have you been the victim of verbal abuse? How does it help to know that God's people (the prophets) have been persecuted throughout history?

Memory Verse: Matthew 5:3–10

9

Disciple

The concept of discipleship is prominent in the New Testament, especially in the Gospels. The word *disciple* (*mathetes*) means "learner." In its narrow technical sense, it refers to someone who has entered into a teacher-student relationship with a rabbi. The term is also used generally to refer to anyone who follows Jesus.

Though discipleship was widely practiced among the Jews, Jesus' calling and relationship to his disciples was unique. It was customary for students to ask a rabbi if they could become his disciples. Instead, Jesus asked his disciples to follow him. This involved a higher level of commitment because Jesus' disciples had to leave everything. In addition to his teachings, Jesus' disciples had to make a commitment to him and his mission of suffering and death (Matthew 16:21; John 15:20).

Shortly after Jesus began his ministry he chose twelve men as disciples, whom he later designated as apostles. Though he had other disciples, the Twelve had a special relationship with Jesus. There was nothing spectacular about the disciples. They were an ordinary lot. Four were fishermen (Mark 1:16–20). Matthew was a despised tax collector (Matthew 9:9). Thomas was a twin and earned the reputation of "the doubter" because he refused to believe in the resurrection unless he actually saw Jesus (John 20:24–25). Simon was a Jewish zealot (Mark 3:18), and Judas betrayed Jesus (John 6:71).

After the beginning of the church, the followers of Christ were called "disciples" (Acts 9:26); but when the church expanded into Gentile areas, they were called "Christians" (Acts 11:25–26). The term *disciple* is not used in the Epistles, probably because the concept of discipleship as practiced by Jesus was no longer possible after his death, resurrection, and ascension. The Holy Spirit replaced Jesus as the "companion" and "teacher" of his followers (John 14:16, 26, my paraphrase), and "elders" as the teachers of the church (1 Timothy 5:17).

Study Questions

1. Mark 1:16–20. These four men left everything to follow Jesus. How would you apply the concept of discipleship today for others and for yourself?
2. Matthew 4:18–22. How is it encouraging to know that the Twelve were common, ordinary men? What does this suggest about the kind of people God uses?
3. John 15:18–25. What kind of antagonism have you experienced because you are a follower of Christ?
4. John 6:60–70.
   a. Why did many of Jesus' disciples desert him?
   b. Why didn't Peter and the other eleven disciples abandon Jesus?
   c. Why do people today turn back from following Jesus?
   d. Why haven't you turned back from following Jesus?
5. Mark 3:19. Why do you think Jesus chose Judas though he knew he would betray him?
6. Acts 11:26. As noted, believers were called Christians rather than disciples when the church expanded into Gentile areas, and the term *disciple* is not used in the Epistles. In addition to the fact that it was no longer physically possible to follow Jesus, more and more women became believers (see Acts 16:13–15). Since in Judaism women were never called disciples, the term apparently wasn't used for women who became followers of Christ.
   a. Is the concept of discipleship valid today, and how would you incorporate it into your church?

b. Why should women be included in a program of discipleship?

Memory Verse: Luke 14:26–27

Feeding of the 5,000

The feeding of the 5,000 is the only miracle recorded in all four Gospels, and it serves a different purpose in each of the Gospels. In Matthew there is an implied reference that Jesus is the prophet like Moses (Deuteronomy 18:15). As Moses provided manna for Israel in the wilderness, Jesus feeds thousands of men, women, and children in a remote area (Matthew 14:13–21).

Though Jesus attempted to find rest in a solitary place, the crowds anticipated where he was going and met him when the boat landed. Mark says that Jesus had compassion on them because he saw them as "sheep without a shepherd" (Mark 6:34). Jesus taught them and multiplied the bread and fish so the disciples could feed 5,000 men and their families (Mark 6:35–44).

Though Jesus had worked miracles and taught about the kingdom of God, people (including the disciples) were still uncertain about his identity. What follows the miracle in Luke's Gospel is the key to its significance. When asked who they thought he was, Peter replied, "You are the Messiah" (Luke 9:20 NLT). This miraculous provision of food for thousands was conclusive evidence that Jesus was from God (Luke 9:10–17).

John gives the longest account of the feeding of the five thousand (John 6:1–15), and adds Jesus' message on "the bread of life" to explain its significance (John 6:22–59). In contrast to Matthew, who uses the Old Testament to show that Jesus fulfilled God's promises, John emphasizes that Jesus exceeded Old Testament expectations. For example, the manna in the wilderness was only a temporary provision, but Jesus is the true bread of heaven, and whoever eats (believes) receives eternal life (John 6:47–51).

Study Questions

1. What are some of the common elements and differences in the four accounts of the feeding of the 5,000?
2. Mark 6:34; Ezekiel 34:1–24. How did Jesus fulfill the prophet's promise?
3. Why did Jesus give the bread and the fish to the disciples to give to the people? What was Jesus trying to teach the disciples? What is the lesson for us today?
4. Why did Jesus pray before multiplying the bread and fish? What does Jesus' example teach us about prayer?
5. Mark 6:41–44; 2 Kings 4:42–44. How is Jesus' miracle different than Elisha's, and how does it show that Jesus was greater and not just another prophet? How would this have impacted people in Jesus' day? How has it affected your view of Jesus?
6. Mark 6:44. Though some claim they can miraculously multiply food today (like mushrooms), why can't we miraculously provide food for people who are starving? What can we do?
7. John 6:14–15. Why do you think Jesus refused to let the people make him king?
8. John 6:59–70. The word *hard* does not mean hard to understand but hard to accept. Why did many desert Jesus, and why didn't the Twelve desert him? Why do people today find it hard to believe in Jesus?
9. John 6:1–70. Jesus fed over 5,000, and then he explained that he was "the bread of life." How can you and/or your church help people with their physical needs and their spiritual need to believe in Jesus as "the bread of life"?

Memory Verse: John 6:47–48

11

God and the Physically Challenged

THE MAN BORN BLIND—JOHN 9

A friend of mine and an outstanding Bible teacher has an adult daughter who lives at home. He and his wife are unbelievably devoted to taking care of her because she cannot completely care for herself. Another friend (I have more than two) and former colleague has a son who is autistic. Though he and his wife have the option of placing their son in an institution, they are lovingly committed to caring for him at home. Like my two friends, almost all of us have been affected by someone with a disability, and we have asked the tough question, "Why?"

Jesus' encounter with a man born blind raises the question of "why?" (John 1:1–5). Jesus and his disciples were in Jerusalem when they saw a man born blind. The disciples asked, "Rabbi, who sinned, this man or his parents, that he was born blind?" (John 9:2). Few today believe that birth defects are the result of sin, but that was a common belief in first-century Judaism. Jesus corrected their misunderstanding, "Neither . . . ," said Jesus, "but this happened so that the works of God might be displayed in him" (John 9:3).

Jesus makes two important points in his answer. First, a congenital handicap is not the result of sin. And second, a disability of any kind creates unique opportunities to glorify God, though it may not be through a miraculous healing.

From a human perspective, especially in our current therapeutic culture, we are inclined to view any condition that puts us at a disadvantage as evil. "Not so," says Jesus. From a divine perspective,

God is sovereign, and it's his will to display his glory through Christ in all circumstances.

Study Questions

1. 2 Samuel 4:4; 9:1–13.
    a. Why did David show kindness to Mephibosheth though he was a descendant of Saul, who had tried to destroy David?
    b. What lessons can we learn about helping those who have disabilities from David's example?

2. Acts 2:45; 4:32–45. Would you include those with disabilities in those helped by the early church? Why or why not?

3. Acts 3:1–11.
    a. Though we can't restore the sight of the blind as Jesus did or heal the handicapped like Peter, what are some of the ways we can help those with disabilities?
    b. What are some of the ways churches can minister to those with special needs?
    c. If your church does not have a special needs ministry, how could you help your church start one?

Theological (Doctrinal) Questions

The story about the man born blind is about those who are both physically and spiritually blind (John 9:1–41).

4. John 9:5. In what sense is Jesus the "light of the world"?

5. John 9:35–41.
    a. Why do you think the blind man believed in Jesus but the religious leaders didn't?
    b. What is worse, physical or spiritual blindness? Why?

6. John 9:3. How can God be glorified through a disability?

—Optional

Commentators disagree on whether this passage teaches that God was the direct cause of the man's blindness or his blindness was the result of natural causes and Jesus used his handicap to glorify God through a miraculous revelation of his deity.

7. What are the strengths and weaknesses of these two views?

8. What is the implication of each of these views for God's sovereignty (absolute control) over all disabilities?

Memory Verse: Romans 8:28

12

Herodians

The Herodians are best known for conspiring with the Pharisees to kill Jesus (Mark 3:6). We don't know their exact origin or what they believed. They were a political not a religious party. Their name comes from combining *Herod* with the suffix *–ianos*, meaning "followers of." They were supporters of Herod the Great ("king of the Jews") and his descendants. The Romans had made the Herods "puppet kings" in Israel, and they were despised by most Jews because they were Edomites or Idumeans, descendants of Esau. But apparently, some Jews favored Herodian rule and were called Herodians.

The Herodians are mentioned only three times in the Gospels (Mark 3:6; 12:13; Matthew 22:16). They considered Jesus a political threat to Roman rule so they plotted with the Pharisees to kill him (Mark 3:6). During Jesus' final week in Jerusalem, the Pharisees and Herodians tried to trap him with an incriminating question (Mark 12:13). What is surprising about the Pharisees and Herodians conspiring together is that the two groups didn't normally associate with each other. They apparently feared and despised Jesus so much they were willing to join forces to destroy him.

Study Questions

1. Matthew 22:15–22.
   a. Why were the Herodians and Pharisees willing to cooperate to trap Jesus with a politically charged question?
   b. Why did the Herodians ask Jesus a question about taxes instead of a religious question?

c. What is the implication of Jesus' answer about a Christian's responsibility to government?

d. Should a Christian pay taxes to a government that oppresses people?

e. What did Jesus mean when he said, "Give to God what belongs to God"? What is the implication for our responsibility to God?

f. Why were the Herodians and Pharisees unable to refute Jesus' answer?

2. Mark 3:1–6.

a. It's not stated, but what do you think the Pharisees said to convince the Herodians to work together to kill Jesus?

b. What made Jesus angry? How would you describe a "hard heart" (NLT)?

c. Do you think Christians have a right to get angry with people? Why or why not?

3. Do you think Christians should get involved in political movements? Why or why not?

Memory Verse: Matthew 22:16–17

13

"I Am"

GOSPEL OF JOHN

The Gospel of John is unique. Matthew, Mark, and Luke (the Synoptics) give a similar account of the life of Christ, but John's story is different. He gives an extensive account of Jesus' conversations with Nicodemus and the woman at the well. He records seven of Jesus' miracles, which he calls "signs." Five of them are not found in the Synoptic Gospels. He also includes seven of Jesus' messages, all unique to his Gospel.

John's style is simple but profound: "I and the Father are one" (John 10:30). John gives an explanatory commentary (interpretation) of important events. After the miracle of turning water to wine, John explains that it "was the first of the signs through which he revealed his glory; and his disciples believed in him" (John 2:11). John uses dualism (light and darkness, above and below, life and death) and symbols (water, light, bread, shepherd, vine) to communicate truth. He brings what is future in the Synoptics into the present. People who believe have eternal life now and those who don't are already condemned (John 3:16–18).

One of his most unique and important features is his perspective on the person and mission of Christ. Jesus is God's one and only Son who has come into the world to reveal the Father (John 1:18). In contrast to the authors of the Synoptic Gospels, it is Jesus himself who claims oneness with his Father and the nature of his mission. Jesus makes seven "I am" statements.

1. "I am the bread of life" (6:35).
2. "I am the light of the world" (8:12; 9:5).
3. "I am the gate for the sheep" (10:7).

4. "I am the good shepherd" (10:11, 14).
5. "I am the resurrection and the life" (11:25).
6. "I am the way and the truth and the life" (14:6).
7. "I am the true vine" (15:1).

Study Questions

1. John 1:18. What are three truths we know about God from the Son?

2. John 6:35. Jesus' promise is about spiritual not physical hunger. How has Christ satisfied your spiritual hunger?

3. John 8:12; 1 John 1:5–7. (Note that John refers to both Jesus and God as light.) Jesus made this statement during the Feast of Tabernacles, a celebration of God's provision for Israel in the wilderness. As part of the festival, the priests lit huge lamps in the Temple as a reminder of God's guidance by a cloud and pillar of fire. How does faith in Christ keep us from walking in darkness?

4. John 10:6–10; see Luke 13:22–30 for a related metaphor in a parable. Jesus is drawing a contrast between himself and Israel's religious leaders (cf. Ezekiel 34:1–6). Who or what are some of the religious thieves in the world today?

5. John 10:11. What characterizes Jesus as a "good shepherd"? See Psalm 23. How has Jesus protected and comforted you?

6. John 11:25–26; Ephesians 2:1–7. What did Jesus mean when he said, "whoever lives by believing in me will never die"? How is it comforting to know that you are spiritually alive and will never die?

7. John 14:6. What are some of the different ways other religions teach as the way to God or to happiness? How

did you try to find fulfillment in life before you trusted in Christ?

8. John 15:1–4. What are your spiritual habits that keep you connected to Jesus?

Memory Verse: Memorize the seven "I am" statements.

14

Jesus and Demons

Jesus' conflict with demons is part of his greater mission to establish the kingdom of God. To establish God's kingdom, it was necessary for Jesus to make a direct assault on the kingdom of Satan. Though Matthew, Mark, and Luke record multiple accounts of Jesus' encounters with demons, this study will be limited to the Gospel of Mark.

Mark records that when Jesus went into Galilee, he announced the arrival of the kingdom (Mark 1:14–15). When Jesus entered a synagogue at Capernaum he was immediately confronted by a demon-possessed man (Mark 1:21–24). Mark identified the demon as "an unclean spirit" (v. 23 ESV) because demons have a contaminating effect on people and creation. The demon called Jesus "the Holy One of God" (v. 24) because he recognized that Jesus was set apart from everything unclean. With a stern and powerful command Jesus silenced the demon and ordered him to come out of the man. The demon immediately obeyed Jesus' command (Mark 1:25–26).

As Jesus traveled throughout Galilee, he preached in their synagogues and drove out demons (Mark 1:39).

Though the context is different than Matthew and Luke, Mark records the charge of the religious leaders that Jesus' power of exorcism was of Satan/Beelzebul (Mark 3:22–30). (Beelzebul or Beelzebub was a popular name for Satan.)

Jesus' mission against the kingdom of Satan extended beyond the borders of Israel. When Jesus went into the region of Gerasenes, a man who was possessed by multiple demons charged Jesus, but instead of attacking he fell on his knees at Jesus' feet. In a surprise move, Jesus forced "the unclean spirits" (Mark 5:13 ESV) to leave the man but allowed them to enter a herd of pigs (animals that the Jews considered unclean). The pigs stampeded over a cliff and drowned in the sea (Mark 5:1–20).

Jesus delivered two children from demon possession. When he traveled north to Tyre, Jesus cast a demon out of the daughter of a Syrophoenician woman (Mark 7:24–30). He freed a boy whom his disciples had been unable to help from an unclean spirit that had mercilessly tormented the boy (Mark 9:14–29).

Study Questions

1. Mark 1:24. At the time of Christ it was thought that naming an opponent in the spiritual conflict was a way of gaining control.
    a. How did the demon attempt to control Jesus, and what was Jesus' response?
    b. Why was the demon(s) afraid of Jesus? (Note the plural "us.")
2. Mark 5:6. Why did the demon-possessed man fall on his knees before Jesus? What does this suggest about the person of Christ?
3. Mark 5:11–13. Why did the demons beg to be sent into a herd of pigs, and why did Jesus allow them to possess the pigs? What happened to the pigs? What does this suggest about the nature of demon possession?
4. Mark 1:27; Luke 4:36. Jesus obviously has authority over unseen evil forces. What does this suggest about the cosmic struggle between God and Satan in creation?
5. Matthew 12:24. Why did the religious leaders charge that Jesus' power was from Satan?
6. Mark 9:20–22. What effect did the "impure spirit" have on the boy? What does this suggest about the intentions of Satan and his demonic forces?

7. Mark 9:17–18, 28–29.
   a. Why couldn't Jesus' disciples cast the demon out of the boy?
   b. What lesson does Jesus teach from this incident (see also Mark 11:22–24)?
   c. What is the lesson for us today?
   d. Why do you think Jesus didn't encourage his disciples to cast out demons but instead taught them a lesson on prayer?

Memory Verse: Mark 1:24

15

Jesus' Miracles

Though some attempt to explain the miracle stories in the Gospels as natural phenomenon or the creation of the early church, conservative Christians believe that they were supernatural events accurately and faithfully recorded by the Gospel writers.

The approximately thirty-five miracles of Jesus recorded in the Gospels can be divided into four categories: healings, exorcisms (casting out demons), nature miracles, and raising the dead.

Though Jesus healed many, he did not heal everyone. Jesus' purpose was to give evidence that he was the promised Christ (Messiah) and that he had come to fulfill God's kingdom promises. When John the Baptist was arrested, he sent his disciples to ask Jesus if he were indeed the promised Messiah. Jesus replied, "Go back and report to John what you hear and see: The blind receive sight, the lame walk, those who have leprosy are cleansed, the deaf hear, the dead are raised, and the good news is proclaimed to the poor" (Matthew 11:4–5; cf. Luke 7:22). Jesus' response is related to promises in the book of Isaiah about the coming of the kingdom and the restoration of creation (Isaiah 35:5–6; 61:1–2). When Jesus healed a man who was demon possessed, blind, and unable to speak, the religious leaders charged that his power was from Beelzebul (a code name for Satan). Jesus answered by claiming the miracle was evidence of the arrival of the kingdom (Matthew 12:22–28).

For this study we will examine one miracle from each of the four categories listed above.

Study Questions

Healings

Mark 2:1–12

1. What was the reaction of the religious leaders to what Jesus did? How did Jesus respond to their criticism?
2. Which do you think was more important, forgiving the man's sins or healing him? Which do you think is more important today? Why?

Exorcisms

Mark 5:1–20

3. What did the demon-possessed man do when Jesus got out of the boat? Why is this significant?
4. Why did Jesus allow the demons to enter a herd of pigs, and what happened to the pigs?
5. What was the reaction of the people living in the area? Do people fear Jesus today? Why?

Nature

Luke 8:22–25

6. How did Jesus' disciples respond to the threat of the storm?
7. Why did the disciples ask, "Who is this?" At this point in their relationship with Jesus do you think they understood that he was both God and man? What features of this miracle story reveal both Jesus' humanity and his deity?

Raising the Dead

Mark 5:21–43

8. A synagogue ruler was the president of the local synagogue, important, and highly respected in the community. What

did the synagogue ruler do when he approached Jesus, and what would the people have thought about what Jairus did?

9. Do you think Jesus would have helped Jairus if he had not knelt and begged him to help his daughter? How did Jesus' response fulfill his mission as Savior?

10. What is the evidence that Jairus's daughter was dead? What does this miracle preview about death?

Optional

11. What does Jesus' calming of the storm reveal about creation that has been corrupted by sin?

12. In the story of the woman who was healed of a bleeding illness, why do you think Jesus made the woman publicly confess that she had touched his cloak? The answer is related to the fact that the woman would have been considered ceremonially unclean by the community.

Memory Verse: Acts 2:22

16

Jesus' Teaching on Prayer

Though the disciples had seen Jesus heal the sick, cure leprosy, cast out demons, feed 5,000, and calm a raging storm, they didn't ask him how to do any of those things. One day after watching Jesus pray, they asked, "Lord, teach us to pray, just as John taught his disciples" (Luke 11:1). Apparently John was also a man of prayer.

Jesus responded with what we know as the "Lord's Prayer" (Luke 11:2–4; Matthew 6:7–14). It is a simple prayer that includes honoring God as a gracious, forgiving, and compassionate heavenly Father, and trusting him for our physical and spiritual needs.

Jesus used two stories (parables) to make two points about how to pray (Luke 11:5–13). In the first parable, Jesus used a bad example to teach a good truth. God is the exact opposite of the man who wouldn't get out of bed to help his friend. His excuse for not helping was contrary to first-century Jewish culture, and would have been considered shameful. God is eager to answer prayer. Jesus doesn't tell us why, but sometimes we need to be persistent in prayer. The encouragement for persistence is not to change God's mind, but to demonstrate and strengthen our confidence in God to meet our needs. In the second parable, Jesus sets up an absurd contrast to teach about the goodness of God. To give a trusting child a snake or scorpion would be a cruel and possibly dangerous prank. God would never give us anything that would harm us. For example, he gives "good gifts" to those who ask (Matthew 7:11). Luke, who emphasizes the ministry of the Spirit, has substituted Holy Spirit for "good gifts" (Luke 11:13). The gift of the Spirit was given to all believers on the Day of Pentecost (Acts 2:1–4).

Study Questions

1. Luke 11:1. Why do you think the disciples asked Jesus to teach them to pray? If you could ask Jesus one question about prayer, what would you ask?
2. Luke 11:2; Matthew 6:9. How can we honor God when we pray?
3. Luke 11:2. Why and how should we pray for the advance of God's kingdom on earth?
4. Luke 11:3. We don't need to ask for a daily provision of food in our twenty-first-century culture, but how would you apply the principle to your practice of prayer?
5. Luke 11:4. Why do you think Jesus included a request for forgiveness and a reminder that we need to forgive others? What is the principle for resolving conflict with other people (believers)?
6. Luke 11:4; James 1:12–14. James teaches that God does not tempt anyone, so "lead us not into temptation" probably means to protect us from sin when we are tempted. In addition to prayer, what are some of the other ways we can avoid sin when tempted?
7. Luke 18:1–8.
    a. Have you asked for something but did not receive it? What should we do when God doesn't answer our prayers?
    b. How would you distinguish between persistence and nagging?
    c. What can we learn about ourselves by steadfastness in praying?

8. Luke 11:11–13; Philippians 4:4–7. Though Paul encourages us to pray about everything, what are some of the reasons God may not answer our prayers?

Memory Verse: Matthew 6:9–13

17

Nicodemus

NEW BIRTH AND THE KINGDOM OF GOD

Nicodemus was a Pharisee (John 3:1). The Pharisees insisted on strict obedience to the law of Moses, and most opposed Jesus because they considered him a lawbreaker. But Nicodemus was different. Impressed by Jesus' teaching and his miracles, he came to Jesus at night to discover for himself if Jesus was Israel's Messiah. Jesus shocked him when he said, "No one can see the kingdom of God unless they are born again" (John 3:3). Nicodemus was confused because he thought that Jesus was referring to a second physical birth (John 3:4).

Jesus explained the necessity of a spiritual birth ("born again") to enter the kingdom of God (John 3:5–8). We don't know Nicodemus's immediate response, but at the Feast of Tabernacles he challenged the Sanhedrin for condemning Jesus without a fair hearing. They insulted Nicodemus, accusing him of being as ignorant as the Galileans (John 7:45–52).

After Jesus' crucifixion, Nicodemus and Joseph of Arimathea risked their lives to ask Pilate for the body of Jesus so they could give him a proper burial. Nicodemus provided seventy-five pounds of expensive ointment—an amount suitable for a royal burial—and they placed Jesus' body in a new tomb (John 19:38–42).

Study Questions

1. John 3:1; Matthew 15:1–9.
   a. We don't have Pharisees today, but how do people today attempt to earn God's favor?

b. Galatians 3:10–14. Why does Paul say it is impossible to save yourself, and how is a person saved?

2. John 3:2. Did Nicodemus come to Jesus at night because he was afraid of criticism or because this was the only time he could speak personally to Jesus? When have you felt ashamed to publicly identify yourself as a Christian?

3. John 3:4. Why is it difficult for unbelievers like Nicodemus to understand spiritual truths?

4. John 3:5–9.
   a. How would you explain what it means to be "born again" to an unbeliever?
   b. The expression "born of water and the Spirit" is commonly thought to refer to physical birth, but a better interpretation is found in Ezekiel 36:25–27. Why is it more likely that Nicodemus would have understood water as a symbol for spiritual cleansing than physical birth?
   c. What does wind symbolize? See Titus 3:4–7.

5. John 7:50–52. How are some unbelievers like the Pharisees who rejected Jesus and ridiculed Nicodemus? How would you respond to people who reject Jesus without considering the evidence?

6. John 19:38–42; 2 Corinthians 8:1–5. What can you do that is extravagant (sacrificial) to help advance the cause of Christ?

Memory Verse: John 3:5

18

Parables of Jesus

Jesus said, "Listen! A farmer went out to sow his seed. As he was scattering the seed, some fell along the path, and the birds came and ate it up. . . ." (Mark 4:3–8). Everyone loves a good story, and that is one of the reasons that Jesus was so popular. He told stories that engaged people, made them think, and were easy to remember. These stories are called parables.

The majority of the parables in the Bible are found in the prophets and the teachings of Jesus. There are no parables in the book of Acts or the Epistles.

In Jesus' day, people understood his stories because they were about life in Israel, but that was a different time and place. To understand them today, we need to pay close attention to several principles. First, we must observe the context. This means reading the passages before and after the parable to determine the audience and the reason for the parable. Second, in the past, it was believed that parables taught only one main point. They were not allegories, in which all of the details have symbolic meaning. Craig Blomberg, however, has made a convincing argument that parables can have more than one main point. To avoid turning them into allegories, he says that parables contain as many main points as primary characters in the parable. In his book *Interpreting the Parables*, he categorizes parables as three-point, two-point, and one-point parables. A final principle: Jesus' stories are primarily about the arrival of God's promised kingdom and what this means for kingdom subjects. Though Jesus never directly identifies himself with any of the characters in his parables, Blomberg has stated in the last section of his book that parables raise questions about the identity of Jesus. Who is he? Is he really the Son of God?

The questions will focus on only one of the approximately thirty-six parables in the Gospels, and guide you through the process of interpreting and applying a parable.

Study Questions

Luke 16:1–13

1. Who is the audience? Is this parable for unbelievers or believers?
2. Why does the rich man plan to fire his financial manager?
3. What does the manager do when he realizes that his boss is going to fire him?
4. Commentators are divided on whether or not what the manager did was dishonest. Some believe the manager had overcharged the debtors and was merely reducing the overcharges or sacrificing his commission. The rich man did not actually lose anything. Because nothing in the parable suggests this, others believe the manager was again acting dishonestly.

   What is the surprising element in the story? What was the rich man's response to what his manager did? Why do you think he did this?
5. The parable ends in verse 9. If Blomberg is correct that there are as many truths as main characters, how many characters are in the parable?
6. What are the three truths of the parable (vv. 10–13)?
7. How does Jesus encourage us to use our worldly resources (wealth)? See Matthew 6:19–21 and 1 Timothy 6:17–19.
8. What do you think it means that if we "can be trusted with very little," we "can also be trusted with much" (v. 10)? The contrast between "little" and "much" most likely refers to

the difference between material possessions of this world and spiritual treasures.

9. What did Jesus mean when he said, "No one can serve two masters. For you will hate one and love the other" (Luke 16:13 NLT)?

10. What is the main message of this parable?

Memory Verse: Mark 4:10–12

19

Pharisees

On what is called "the Day of Controversy," Jesus was challenged by the Jewish religious establishment—Pharisees and Sadducees (Matthew 23). Neither of these religious groups are referenced in the Old Testament. They both developed during the turbulent years between the Testaments. The Pharisees were the chief opponents of Jesus (Gospels), and the Sadducees of the early church (Acts).

If not mentioned in the Old Testament, what is the origin of the Pharisees? When the Seleucids (Greeks) controlled Israel from 198–142 BC, they tried to force the Jews to give up their traditions and adopt Greek customs. The Jews who resisted were known as the Hasidim or "the pious ones." Their fanatical and strict lifestyle was carried on by the Pharisees or "the separate ones," who considered themselves the watchdogs of the law of Moses. They hated Jesus because he exposed their hypocritical legalism. It is important to note that Jesus did not break the law of Moses. He said that he came to fulfill the Law not destroy it (Matthew 5:17). Jesus ignored the Pharisees' application of the Law (oral traditions), which he considered an absurd burden, and insisted on the righteous application of the Law (Matthew 5:20). Another point to note is that not all Pharisees were hypocrites. Nicodemus, a godly Pharisee, respected Jesus as a teacher and after the crucifixion helped Joseph of Arimathea bury Jesus (John 3:1–2; 19:38–39).

Study Questions

1. Matthew 5:20. What did Jesus mean when he said a person can't enter the kingdom of heaven unless their righteousness exceeds that of the scribes and Pharisees? Was

he talking about keeping more rules or a different kind of righteousness?

2. Matthew 23:1–4. What are some of the expectations we impose on people that hinder rather than help their relationship with God?

3. Mark 2:23–28. The disciples were not stealing grain. According to the Pharisees' interpretation of the Law, they were working by rubbing the chaff from the kernel. How does Jesus' answer influence your view of Sunday or the day you worship?

4. Mark 3:1–6. How and why do you think legalism breeds hatred and malice?

5. Luke 7:36–50. What are some similar situations today where individuals and churches are criticized for associating with unbelievers (sinners)? How would Jesus respond?

6. Matthew 15:1–11. What are some of the traditions practiced by churches that should be abandoned?

7. Luke 15:1–2. In response to the Pharisees who criticized him for speaking and even eating with sinners, Jesus told three parables to emphasize the love of God (Luke 15:3–32). How would you respond to someone who criticizes believers for associating with sinners?

8. John 9:13–16. After Jesus healed the man who had been born blind, the Pharisees stubbornly refused to believe because Jesus had healed him on the Sabbath. Why do people today refuse to believe in Jesus in spite of the evidence that he is the Son of God?

9. Matthew 9:9–13. How does Jesus' response to the Pharisees who criticized him for eating with sinners at Matthew's house affect your view of unbelievers?

10. Acts 23:1–10. How did Paul cause a debate between the Pharisees and Sadducees that was so volatile that the Romans had to rescue him from the Sanhedrin?

Memory Verse: Matthew 5:20

20

Sanhedrin

The Sanhedrin was a Jewish tribunal comprised of seventy members plus the high priest. The majority of the members were wealthy Sadducees but some were Pharisees (John 11:47; Acts 23:6). They had the authority over internal affairs, especially alleged violations of the law of Moses.

According to Jewish tradition the origin of the Sanhedrin goes back to Moses' choosing of seventy elders to help with complaints (Numbers 11:16). During the time of Ezra and Nehemiah, a council of elders had limited authority over affairs related to the Temple and Jerusalem (Ezra 5:3–5; Nehemiah 2:16). The Sanhedrin of New Testament times apparently came into existence during the Greek period and continued as the governing body of the Jews through the Roman period. The Sanhedrin ceased to exist when the Romans destroyed Jerusalem in AD 70.

The Romans granted the Sanhedrin significant power over matters related to the law of Moses and the Temple. After the raising of Lazarus, the Sanhedrin became alarmed at Jesus' soaring popularity. Caiaphas, the high priest, recommended the Sanhedrin get rid of him (John 11:49–57), but they were afraid to arrest him publicly (Matthew 21:46). Just before Passover, temple guards arrested Jesus at night and took him to Annas, who was the former high priest but had been removed from office by the Romans (John 18:12–24). Annas questioned Jesus, and then sent him to Caiaphas, his son-in-law and the actual high priest (John 18:24). After questioning Jesus, the full Sanhedrin found him guilty of blasphemy (Matthew 26:65–66). Because they apparently didn't have the authority to impose the death penalty, they turned Jesus over to Pilate on charges of sedition (John 18:31; Matthew 27:1–2).

After the resurrection the Sanhedrin continued their opposition to the Jesus movement. The Sadducees ordered Peter and John arrested, and the Sanhedrin warned them to stop teaching about the resurrection (Acts 4:1–22). Because of the apostles' popularity with the people all were arrested and flogged (Acts 5:17–42). Though the Sanhedrin didn't have the authority for capital punishment, they were able to stone Stephen to death (Acts 7:1–60). When Paul appeared before the Sanhedrin, he insulted the high priest and caused a violent argument between the Pharisees and Sadducees over the resurrection (Acts 23:1–10). A group of forty fanatical Jews conspired with the high council to assassinate Paul (Acts 23:12–15).

Study Questions

1. John 11:45–54.
   a. Why did Caiaphas recommend that the Sanhedrin get rid of Jesus?
   b. Why do people today want to remove Christianity from the public arena?

2. Luke 22:66–71.
   a. Why did the high council refuse to believe that Jesus was the Messiah and Son of God?
   b. What are the reasons people today refuse to believe that Jesus is the Son of God?

3. Mark 14:53–59.
   a. What was the problem with the testimony of the witnesses against Jesus?
   b. Why do you think the Sanhedrin was willing to condemn Jesus though they knew the witnesses were lying?

4. Acts 4:13–15.
   a. Why was the council surprised by the boldness of Peter and John?

b. How does their courage encourage you when you are challenged by unbelievers?

c. How would you counsel a high school student who says he or she is sometimes ridiculed for being a believer?

5. Acts 5:33–39. The council was so infuriated by the apostles, they planned to kill them. But a Pharisee named Gamaliel defended them.

   a. Why did he say the council should leave them alone?

   b. What do you think of his advice?

   c. How does the story in the book of Acts support Gamaliel's argument? See Acts 28:30–31.

Memory Verse: John 15:18–19

21

Scribes/Teachers of the Law

I was a teacher with the title Professor of Bible for over thirty-five years. Students occasionally called me "Scribe Marty." Had I lived in Israel in the first century, that would have been my official title. Scribes were experts in the law of Moses. They had devoted themselves to the study of the Law so they could teach others.

Though scribes are mentioned early in the Old Testament story, most believe the scribal tradition of teaching the Law began with Ezra. According to Ezra 7:10, he devoted himself to the study and personal application of the Law and to teaching others.

During the time of Christ, scribes were not a separate religious movement but members of the two main religious parties. Most scribes were Pharisees, but some belonged to the party of the Sadducees. Though the tradition from Ezra of studying, obeying, and teaching the Law was noble, like the Pharisees and Sadducees, many scribes were religious hacks. Jesus denounced them as hypocrites and called them "blind guides" because what they taught misrepresented the intent of the Law (Matthew 23:1–36). They considered Jesus a renegade Jew because he ignored their application of the law of Moses. For example, they were offended because Jesus ate with people they despised (Mark 2:15–16), and they complained about Jesus' disciples because they didn't ceremonially wash their hands (Matthew 15:1–2).

Study Questions

1. Matthew 23:13–14. In addition to the scribes missing the kingdom of heaven, what did Jesus warn was the other danger of false teaching? What do some religious groups teach

today that is erroneous and will prevent people from trusting Christ as Savior?

2. Luke 20:45–47. Why did Jesus warn his disciples about the scribes? God has always encouraged compassion for widows because they are the most vulnerable in society. Who are the most vulnerable in society today, and what can we do to help?

3. Ezra 7:10. What was Ezra's method for studying and teaching the Law (Scriptures)? Note: How does Ezra refer to the Law?
    a. Why is it important that we keep in mind that we are studying the Word of God ("the Law of the Lord") when we study the Bible?
    b. Why and how should we follow Ezra's example in our personal Bible study?
    c. Why is it important to make personal application before teaching others?

4. James 3:1–2. Why does James give a word of caution about becoming a teacher?

5. Matthew 23:16–22. Jesus sternly condemns the scribes. What is the implication of Jesus' condemnation for matters of integrity and keeping our word?

6. Matthew 23:23–28. In this passage, what are the three charges Jesus makes against the scribes and Pharisees?
    a. In verse 24, what did Jesus mean when he said the scribes are careful to strain gnats out of their water but swallow a camel? A clever and funny illustration, but how do we often do the same today?
    b. In verses 25–28, what is Jesus' emphasis in the illustrations (figures of speech) he uses?
    c. Are we like the scribes, giving more time to our outward appearance than internal righteousness? How will

Jesus' warning affect the amount of time you spend in the spiritual dimension of your relationship with the Lord?

Memory Verse: Ezra 7:10

22

Sermon on the Mount

The Sermon on the Mount, which was Jesus' first public message, was a powerful, in-your-face confrontation with Israel's religious elite (Matthew 5–7; Luke 6:17–49). The Pharisees defined righteousness by what you did; Jesus defined it by what you are. When Jesus warned, "Unless your righteousness surpasses that of the Pharisees and teachers of the law, you will certainly not enter the kingdom of heaven" (Matthew 5:20), he wasn't imposing more laws on people. It was a different kind of righteousness—one that comes from the inside out. It was righteousness defined by Jesus—a "Jesus righteousness."

Matthew gives a longer version of the Sermon than Luke. Matthew says that Jesus preached from a "mountainside" (5:1). Luke 6:17 says Jesus spoke on a "plain" (KJV) or a "level area" (NLT). Both writers record the same sermon from different perspectives.

Most agree that the unifying theme is righteousness. Some believe this is the righteousness of God given to believers when they trust Christ as Savior. It's what theologians refer to as "imputed righteousness" and gives believers "a right standing before God." It is this aspect of "righteousness" that Paul emphasizes in Romans. But I think in the Sermon on the Mount it is better to view it as "moral righteousness" or "lifestyle righteousness"—right behavior. It is probably unwise to insist on an absolute separation of the two since it is impossible to live in a way that is pleasing to God without an infusion of his righteousness.

I have found it helpful to organize the Sermon in Matthew into three major sections with an introduction and conclusion.

Setting (5:1–2)
Introduction: The Beatitudes (5:3–12)—The nature of true righteousness
Expectations in relation to the world (5:13–16)
Expectations in relation to the Law (5:17–48)
Expectations in relation to the Father (6:1–7:12)
Conclusion: Two Options (7:13–27)
Response (7:28)

Study Questions

Beatitudes

The term blessed *means "fortunate." A clarifying paraphrase is "approved" by God.*

1. Matthew 5:3. Why does God honor those who are "poor in spirit"?
2. Matthew 5:8. How would you describe a pure heart?
3. Matthew 5:11. How is Jesus' promise comforting for those who are persecuted?

Expectations in relation to the world

4. Matthew 5:13. Jesus uses *salt* as a figure of speech for a preservative. What are some of the ways believers can be salt in the world?

Expectations in relation to the Law

5. Matthew 5:17. The "Law [and] the Prophets" refers to the entire Old Testament. What did Jesus mean when he said he came to fulfill the Law and the Prophets?
6. Matthew 5:21–47. This section is commonly referred to as the antitheses because Jesus contrasts his teaching with the religious leaders' interpretation of Old Testament Law.

Jesus obviously uses hyperbole or exaggeration, but in all of the contrasts he demands a righteousness that exceeds that of the religious leaders.

a. What would change in your community if people were to follow Jesus' teaching?
b. Which of the six antitheses is the most challenging for you?
c. Matthew 5:48. This verse gives a summary principle of Jesus' teaching in the antitheses. How would you apply this principle to a current situation?

Expectations in relation to the Father

In this section Jesus emphasizes the importance of practicing righteousness to please God rather than impress people.

7. Matthew 6:19–24. How can we balance sensible planning for the future with selfish hoarding of our material possessions (wealth)?

8. Matthew 6:25–34. How does Jesus' teaching help you cope with worry?

Conclusion: Two Options

9. Matthew 7:15–20. What do our actions reveal about faith and works?

10. Matthew 7:21–23. What is the ultimate test for a genuine follower of Christ?

Memory Verse: Matthew 5:48

23

Holy Spirit and Jesus

In the Old Testament the Spirit of God was active in creation (Genesis 1:2). The Spirit was given to Israel's leaders to inspire them with courage and strength (Judges 3:10; 6:34; 11:29; 13:25), but was not a permanent gift. The Spirit came upon both Saul and David when they were anointed as Israel's king (1 Samuel 10:10; 16:13). But the Spirit left Saul because of his disobedience (1 Samuel 16:14), and David pleaded with the Lord not to take his Spirit from him when he confessed his sin with Bathsheba (Psalm 51:11). The prophets looked forward to a time when the Spirit would cleanse people from their sins and transform their hearts (Ezekiel 36:25–27). Joel promised that the Spirit would be given to everyone: "I will pour out my Spirit on all people" (Joel 2:28–29).

In the New Testament, the Spirit also had an empowering ministry. An angel announced that John the Baptist would be filled with the Spirit (Luke 1:15). Both of John's parents were filled with the Holy Spirit (Luke 1:41, 67). The role of the Spirit in the virgin birth is a mystery. The angel Gabriel announced to Mary that she would conceive by the power of the Holy Spirit (Luke 1:35).

Matthew, Mark, and Luke focus on the Spirit's ministry to Jesus. Jesus was anointed with the Spirit at his baptism (Luke 3:21–22). He was filled with the Holy Spirit and led by the Spirit when he was tempted by Satan (Luke 4:1–2). The Spirit did not leave Jesus after his victory over Satan, but continued to empower him for his mission (Luke 4:14; Acts 10:38). Jesus' ministry in the power of the Spirit was evidence of the arrival of the age and God's kingdom (Luke 4:18–19; Matthew 12:28).

The Gospel of John also reveals that the kingdom was being fulfilled in the ministry of Jesus. Jesus told Nicodemus that no one could enter the kingdom of God unless they were "born again" (spiritually renewed) (John 3:3–7). At the last Passover meal with his disciples, Jesus anticipated the gift of the Spirit to all believers: "And I will ask the Father, and he will give you another advocate to help you and be with you forever—the Spirit of truth" (John 14:16–17). Jesus also revealed that the Spirit would have a ministry to unbelievers, convicting them of sin, righteousness, and judgment to come (John 16:8–11). After his resurrection, Jesus breathed on his disciples and said, "Receive the Holy Spirit" (John 20:22).

Study Questions

1. Luke 4:1–2. How does the Holy Spirit help us to resist temptation?
2. Luke 4:14. Why did Jesus need the Holy Spirit for ministry since he was the Son of God?
3. John 3:3–8. What does it mean to be "born of the water and the Spirit"? Most commentators do not think Jesus was referring to natural birth and spiritual birth. The best interpretation comes from Ezekiel 36:25–27. See also Titus 3:4–7.
4. John 16:5–11. Why is the ministry of the Holy Spirit crucial in our witness?
5. John 14:15–17. Why did Jesus promise to send the Holy Spirit ("another advocate")? Why do we need the Spirit?

Optional

6. John 20:22. How is the imagery of breathing on the disciples similar to the creation of Adam (Genesis 2:7)? How does this event foreshadow the work of the Spirit in making you a new person in Christ (2 Corinthians 3:16–18; 5:17)?

Memory Verse: John 14:16–17

Olivet Discourse

JESUS' TEACHING ABOUT THE FUTURE

Jesus was not only a king and priest, he was also a prophet. He predicted his death and resurrection on numerous occasions, and he predicted what would happen to Israel in the future. Jesus knew that the power politics of the religious leaders spelled DOOM with capital letters!

It was Thursday, "the day of controversy." Jesus had spent the day teaching in Jerusalem and had been repeatedly harassed by the religious leaders. As they were leaving the temple area, Jesus' disciples looked back in awe and said, "Look, Teacher! What massive stones! What magnificent buildings!" (Mark 13:1). They were right. With its massive white stones that had been polished and decorated with gold, the temple was an architectural wonder. One of the stones in the base weighed approximately 600 tons. No other temple in the ancient world rivaled Herod's temple in size and beauty. Jesus' prediction of its destruction was shocking: "Not one stone here will be left on another; every one will be thrown down" (Mark 13:2). The disciples incredulously asked, "When will these things happen? And what will be the sign that they are all about to be fulfilled?" Jesus' answer is known as the "Olivet Discourse" or "Teaching about the Future." The discourse is recorded by Matthew, Mark, and Luke. We will use the message as recorded in Mark for this study (Mark 13:1–37).

Theologians have different views on the fulfillment of Jesus' prophecy. I take the view that Jesus is describing two separate periods of time. The suffering leading up to the destruction of Jerusalem in AD 70 foreshadows the time of unparalleled tribulation at the end of the present age culminating with the second coming of Christ. Like many Old Testament prophecies, Jesus does not clearly reveal a long interval between the destruction of Jerusalem and a time of tribulation prior to his second coming.

The most puzzling and controversial reference is to "the abomination [sacrilege] that causes desolation" (Mark 13:14; Matthew 24:15). It is based on a prophecy in Daniel 9:26–27 and 11:31–32, which was historically fulfilled when Antiochus Epiphanes captured Jerusalem and sacrificed a pig on the temple altar (167 BC). A similar sacrilege happened again in AD 70 when the Romans breached the city's defenses and defiled the temple with their pagan standards. Those historical events foreshadow the ultimate fulfillment when a person identified as the Antichrist will proclaim himself God in the temple (2 Thessalonians 2:3–4, 8–9; Revelation 13:1–10).

Study Questions

1. Mark 13:3–4. What questions would you have asked Jesus?
2. Mark 13:5–11. How should we (believers) respond to claims that current events are signs of Jesus' imminent return?
3. Mark 13:21. How would you respond to a person who says that he is the Messiah?
4. Mark 13:34–37.
   a. Why is it important to remember Jesus' promise to come again?
   b. What is involved in "keeping watch"?
5. Luke 21:34–35. How can we avoid getting so entangled in the affairs of this life that we are not prepared for the Lord's return?
6. 1 Thessalonians 5:1–11.
   a. Why will unbelievers be surprised by the Lord's return? What will happen to them?

   b. Though we don't know the exact time of Christ's return, how should we prepare?
   c. How can we encourage one another concerning Christ's second coming?

7. Revelation 22:20. Are you eagerly anticipating the Lord's return? Why or why not?

Memory Verse: Mark 13:32–33

25

But That's Not Fair

PARABLE OF THE WORKERS

Jesus was a master teacher and used a variety of methods to teach about the kingdom of God. One of his favorites was the parable (a story). Most of Jesus' parables are easy to understand (or accept), but some are hard like the parable of the workers (Matthew 20:1–16).

The parable is both intriguing and troubling. It was harvest season, so the landowner went early in the morning to the local worker pool to hire day laborers. He hired some early in the morning for a denarius—the wage for a full day of work. He hired more at nine, noon, and three, promising to pay them "whatever is right." No problem! At five, he went back to the labor pool to hire more. He fortunately found some who hadn't been hired, so he hired them. No problem! When it was time to pay at the end of the day, the landowner paid all of the workers one denarius, even those who were hired last. Problem! Those who had worked all day complained that it was not fair to pay those who had only worked one hour the same as those who worked all day. The landowner didn't buy it! He had paid them the agreed-upon wage, so he told the complainers it was his money and he could do with it whatever he wanted.

We would agree that what the landowner did wasn't fair—that is, if the point of the story was about workers and wages. But the parable is about the kingdom of heaven (Matthew 20:1). It's about God's abundant grace. Everyone is welcome in the kingdom, and it's never too late to enter.

Study Questions

1. Matthew 20:1. What is the message in this parable about the kingdom of heaven?
2. Matthew 20:4. What does the landowner's statement about paying everyone "whatever is right" imply about the justice of God? How does this parable apply to how employers treat employees today?
3. Matthew 20:11–12.
   a. What are the parallels between workers in this parable and the elder and younger brothers in the parable of the prodigal son (Luke 15:11–32)?
   b. How are we like the workers who complained about the inequity of paying everyone the same?
   c. What are the dangers of resentment, and how can we avoid it?
4. Matthew 20:1–7; Romans 3:23–24, 4:4–5. What does the hiring of workers at different times and paying them all the same wage reveal about God's grace?
5. How does this parable reinforce the truth all people are of equal value, and that all who respond to God's gracious invitation will be accepted into the kingdom?
6. How would you use this parable to assure a person who thinks they are not worthy to be saved that they matter to God?

Memory Verse: Ephesians 2:8–9

26

Prayers of Jesus

Prayer is communication with God. We pray because we believe in God and believe that he hears our prayers. Like a loving parent who is delighted when a child comes to them for help, God is delighted when we acknowledge our dependence on him in prayer. I fully understand why we need to pray, but I've often wondered why Jesus needed to pray if he was God and could do anything. The answer is rather obvious. Jesus was also a man and was dependent on his Father for help.

The Gospels reveal Jesus' practice of prayer. In his high priestly prayer, Jesus prayed for himself, his disciples, and all future believers (John 17). He taught his disciples how to pray (Matthew 6:7–15). On the night he was betrayed Jesus fell to the ground and in great agony of soul asked God to take away the cup of suffering but submitted his will to the sovereign will of his Father (Matthew 26:36–46; Mark 14:32–40; Luke 22:39–44). All four Gospel writers record Jesus' words (prayer) from the cross (Matthew 27:46; Mark 15:34; Luke 23:34; John 19:30).

For this study we will focus on the Gospel of Luke. Luke emphasizes that Jesus was a man of prayer and records nine prayers of Jesus and three parables about prayer.

Study Questions

1. Luke 3:21. What do you think Jesus prayed?

2. Luke 5:16. Why is it important that we pray often in solitude? Do you have a special place and take the time to meet regularly with the Lord? If not, I encourage you to consider

making a special place and time for prayer. It could be your favorite chair.

3. Luke 6:12.
    a. Why did Jesus pray all night before choosing the Twelve?
    b. Though not many of us have the spiritual discipline to pray all night, why should we pray before making important decisions? If you are considering a major decision, how much time have you spent seeking God's will?
    c. What are some of the ways God guides us in decision-making?

4. Luke 9:18. The context and occasion suggest this was impromptu prayer. What are some of the reasons why we might want to pause in our daily activities (routine) for prayer? Is this something we should do?

5. Luke 9:28–29. Do you think Jesus would have been transformed if he had not been praying? I doubt if God's glory will be revealed in us the same way it was in Jesus, but how might we be changed by prayer?

6. Luke 11:1–4. How has Jesus' example of prayer motivated you to pray?

7. Luke 21:36. From the context it seems that Jesus is instructing believers to pray for strength to keep from sinning. How often do you pray that you may stand approved when Christ returns? (See 1 John 3:1–3.)

8. Luke 22:32. What can we learn about praying for others from Jesus' praying for Peter? If you know someone who is struggling with an issue, how can you pray for them?

9. Luke 23:34. It is remarkable that Jesus prayed for his executioners. If someone has hurt you, will you ask God to forgive them, and will you forgive them?

—Parables (Optional)

10. Luke 11:5–13. These two parables emphasize persistence in prayer and the goodness of God. How do we distinguish between persistence and nagging God for requests that are not his will?
11. Luke 18:1–8. How does prayer help us withstand persecution (difficulties)?

Memory Verse: Matthew 6:9–13.

If you haven't already done so, I encourage you to memorize the Lord's Prayer (which is actually the disciples' prayer).

27

Transfiguration

The transfiguration is recorded in Matthew (17:1–9), Mark (9:2–10), and Luke (9:28–36) but not John. Since the transfiguration is a revelation of Jesus' glory, it is probable that John didn't record it because his entire Gospel is a revelation of Jesus' glory.

Immediately after Peter identified Jesus as the Messiah, Jesus shocked the Twelve when he announced that he would be rejected and killed (Mark 8:29–33). They anticipated that the Messiah would overthrow the hated Romans and restore the kingdom to Israel; instead Jesus predicted that he had come to die and rise again. Since they didn't understand what Jesus meant by a resurrection, their dreams were shattered. To reassure the Twelve that he was the Messiah and Son of God, Jesus took Peter, James, and John with him to a high mountain, where he gave them a glimpse of his glory that was concealed by his humanity (Mark 9:1–10).

I used to teach students that Jesus pulled aside his humanity so the three could see his deity, but after several years I realized my explanation was misleading. I missed a critical point in the event. I was making a distinction between Jesus' deity and his humanity; but once Jesus took on a human body (incarnation), his essence was changed so he became inseparably both God and man. What happened at the transfiguration was a miraculous transformation (metamorphosis) of Jesus' humanity to reveal his divine glory now veiled in a body of flesh.

Study Questions

1. Matthew 17:1. Why didn't Jesus take all of the Twelve with him to a high mountain?

2. Matthew 17:1. Mount Tabor is the traditional location for the transfiguration. Mount Hermon and Mount Merom are other possibilities. Why did Jesus reveal his glory on a mountain? What event in the Old Testament is the background for this revelation of glory? See Exodus 33:18–23. What is the main difference between the event in Exodus 33 and Matthew 17?

3. Mark 6:3. What future event does the transfiguration preview? See 2 Corinthians 3:16–18. How do you think this revelation of God's glory affected Jesus' followers? How did it assure them that Jesus was the Son of God? How does it affect your view of Christ?

4. 2 Corinthians 3:16–18. How does knowing that we will one day be completely transformed and glorified strengthen your faith for the present and give you hope for the future?

5. Mark 9:4. What two individuals appeared with Jesus and why?

6. Mark 9:5–6. What was the problem with Peter's suggestion that they build three shelters?

7. Mark 9:7. God's command to listen is from Deuteronomy 18:15, a passage that promises a prophet like Moses. In the context of Mark 8:31–33, why did God give this command?

8. Mark 9:9–10. What didn't the disciples understand? When would they fully understand what Jesus meant? Why is it so difficult for people to accept the resurrection?

Optional

9. Mark 9:1. What did Jesus mean when he said, "Some who are standing here will not taste death before they see that the kingdom of God has come with power"? Four proposed

views of what the kingdom coming with power looks like are as follows:

a. The transfiguration, which was a preview of Jesus' kingdom glory
b. Jesus' resurrection and ascension
c. The coming of the Holy Spirit at Pentecost
d. The second coming of Christ to establish the eternal kingdom of God

Of the four, which do you think is the best option? I think the context favors the first, but it's okay if you disagree.

Memory Verse: Matthew 17:5–6

28

Greatness of Christ

THE USE OF THE OLD TESTAMENT IN THE GOSPEL OF JOHN

The coming of Jesus was anticipated. The writers of the New Testament are quick to point out how Jesus fulfills messianic promises in the Old Testament.

For Matthew Jesus is the Davidic Messiah, but he is more. When asked what he believed about Jesus, Peter confessed, "You are the Christ [Messiah], the Son of the Living God" (Matthew 16:16 NLT). As Messiah and the Son of God Jesus is the complete and final fulfillment of specific Old Testament passages.

Luke portrays Jesus as the fulfillment of the history of salvation, a plan that is inclusive of everyone. In his description of the ministry of John the Baptist, Luke quotes a passage from Isaiah that ends with a universal dimension: "And all people will see God's salvation" (Luke 3:6).

Mark focuses on the establishment of the kingdom. But Jesus inaugurates the kingdom to overthrow Satan, not to fulfill Old Testament prophecies. In fact, Jesus' identity is a "messianic secret" that is progressively revealed.

John's use of the Old Testament is different than the other three Gospels. His primary purpose is evangelistic. He wants people to believe that Jesus is the Christ and Son of God (John 20:30–31). He doesn't use specific quotes from the Old Testament (Matthew), a promise-fulfillment paradigm (Luke), or a kingdom theme (Mark). Instead, he uses analogies and shows how Jesus exceeds the Old Testament person or event.

Study Questions

1. John 1:16–18; Exodus 33:12–23. How does Jesus exceed Moses? What has knowing about Jesus revealed to you about God?

2. John 3:13–15; Numbers 21:4–9.
   a. Though people didn't die immediately, what eventually happened to those who looked at the "bronze serpent" in the wilderness? What do those who believe in Jesus receive?
   b. How would you explain what it means to "believe in Jesus"? How is believing different than knowing about Jesus?

3. John 4:10–14; Psalm 42:1. The water Jesus promised was fresh flowing water from a spring, not stagnant water from a cistern. What is the gift of God? We satisfy our physical thirst with water; how do we satisfy our spiritual thirst?

4. John 6:14, 32–33, 46–52, 58; Exodus 16:1–5; Deuteronomy 18:15. The feeding of the 5,000 reminded the people of Moses and the provision of manna in the wilderness.
   a. How does Jesus surpass Moses?
   b. What does it mean to eat the bread of life? Unlike physical bread, which we need to eat regularly, why do we need to eat the bread of life only one time?

5. John 7:37–39; 1 Corinthians 6:19; Titus 3:4–7. One of the rituals at the Feast of Tabernacles was the pouring out of water from the Gihon Spring on the temple altar as a reminder of God's provision in the wilderness. When did you receive the Holy Spirit and how does he function in your life?

6. John 8:12; 9:5; Numbers 9:15–23. As a reminder of how God was with them in the wilderness, the priests lit giant

lamps in the temple during the Feast of Tabernacles. What does it mean to walk in light rather than darkness?

7. John 10:11–18. What are some of the ways Christ, "the Good Shepherd," cares for you today?

8. John 15:1–8; Psalm 80; Isaiah 5:1–7; Galatians 5:22–23. Israel was God's chosen vine, but the nation had become fruitless. Jesus fulfills what God hoped for Israel. How do you remain (abide) connected to Jesus (the "true vine")?

Memory Verse: John 6:35

29

Woman at the Well

One of the ways John tells the story of Jesus is through conversations (dialogue between two people). The story of the woman at the well is a classic in Christianity (John 4:1–42).

After an initial season of ministry in Jerusalem, Jesus left for the province of Galilee. It was not surprising that Jesus decided to go to Galilee. Jesus had grown up in Galilee, and all of his disciples were from Galilee. But the route Jesus chose was a surprise. Instead of bypassing Samaria, Jesus walked directly north on a route that took him through the village of Sychar.

In Sychar, Jesus met a woman who had come to draw water from the town well. He captured her attention by asking for a drink. His question was surprising (shocking) because Jews and Samaritans despised one another. The animosity between Jews and Samaritans went back hundreds of years to the resettlement of the Northern Kingdom after the Assyrians had conquered it. The Assyrians repopulated the area with mixed races of people, and the Jews who remained intermarried and assimilated some of the religious and cultural practices of the foreigners. Their descendants were known as Samaritans. By Jesus' time the region of Samaria was sandwiched between Judea in the south and Galilee in the north.

Jesus quickly turned the conversation to spiritual matters by declaring that he could give her "living water" and was offering her "eternal life." She was confused but asked for the water. Jesus exposed her spiritual need by telling her to call her husband. The woman denied that she had a husband, but Jesus knew that she had been married five times. She thought Jesus must be a prophet and asked if people should worship at the Samaritan temple on Mount Gerizim or at the Jewish temple in Jerusalem. Jesus replied that the place didn't matter: "God is spirit, and those who worship him must worship in spirit and truth" (John 4:24 ESV). She then thought that Jesus might be the Messiah the Samaritans were expecting. Jesus' reply is the only time that he stated directly that he was the Messiah: "I, the one speaking to you—I am he" (John 4:26).

The woman then returned to town and told everyone what had happened. They rushed out to see Jesus and discovered for themselves that Jesus was indeed the Savior of the world.

Study Questions

1. John 4:4–5; Acts 1:8; 8:4–25. The expression, "Now he had to go through Samaria," means it was a divine necessity.
    a. Why was it necessary for Jesus to go through Samaria?
    b. Who are some of the people we isolate and neglect and why?
    c. How can we develop a godly concern for those who are despised and isolated?
2. John 4:7–9. Who are the people in your community that others avoid? How can you and your church reach out to them?
3. John 4:10–15. When talking to unbelievers, what are some of the ways we can refocus the conversation on spiritual matters?
4. John 4:16–18. What are some of the moral barriers that keep people from admitting their spiritual need?
5. John 4:19–24. What does it mean to worship in "spirit and truth" (ESV)?
6. John 4:25–26. Though the Samaritans identified the Messiah by a different name, they believed he would have divine insight, so the woman concluded Jesus might be the one

they were expecting. What do you think is the most compelling reason to believe that Jesus is the Son of God?

7. John 4:31–38. Jesus received spiritual nourishment by doing the will of God. How do you nourish your spiritual life?

8. John 4:39–42. The conclusion that Jesus was indeed the Savior of the world is remarkable. Even the Jews did not have that kind of universal understanding of Jesus' mission. What can we do to maintain or develop a universal perspective on mission?

Memory Verse: John 4:42

30

Zacchaeus

"CHIEF TAX COLLECTOR"

There is a favorite children's song about "a wee little man" named Zacchaeus.

> Zacchaeus was a wee little man,
> A wee little man was he,
> He climbed up in the sycamore tree,
> For the Lord he wanted to see,
> And as the Savior passed that way,
> He looked up in the tree,
> And he said, "Zacchaeus, you come down,
> For I'm going to your house for tea."

No one likes taxes. We don't, and the Jews in the first century didn't. They despised tax collectors because they were collaborators with the Romans. Tax collectors made a profit by collecting more in taxes than they had to pay the Romans. Zacchaeus was a "chief tax collector" (Luke 19:2), making him even more despised than the subordinate collectors who worked for him, but his position had also made him extremely rich.

We don't know why he was so determined to see Jesus. But when the Lord came to Jericho, Zacchaeus had a problem. He was so short he had to climb a tree to see over the crowds that lined the road (Luke 19:1–4).

It was both surprising and embarrassing when Jesus stopped and spoke to Zacchaeus (Luke 19:5). It was surprising that Jesus would speak to a man hated by the Jews, and it was embarrassing to a wealthy tax collector that all eyes were fixed on him in a tree. By inviting himself to the home of Zacchaeus Jesus was affirming God's love for the outsider, a common theme in the Gospel of Luke.

Zacchaeus's response emphasizes one of the major themes of Luke's Gospel—repentance. Zacchaeus offered to help the poor and repay those he had cheated. The Lord commended Zacchaeus as a true "son of Abraham," and declared that he had come "to seek and to save" people like Zacchaeus (Luke 19:7–10).

Study Questions

1. Luke 19:3–4.
   a. Luke 18:9–14. What is Jesus' point about humility in the parable of the Pharisees and tax collector?
   b. How is Zacchaeus a real-life example of the tax collector in the parable?
   c. How important is humility in coming to faith in Christ?
2. Luke 19:5–7.
   a. How does the contrast between Jesus' response to Zacchaeus and that of the people remind us that outsiders are valuable to God?
   b. What can you do to help an outsider know that they matter to God?
3. Luke 19:8.
   a. The Law required a twenty percent penalty for damages to another person's property (Leviticus 5:16; Num. 5:7). Why do you think Zacchaeus offered to give half of his wealth to the poor and repay fourfold those he had cheated? Was Zacchaeus trying to earn his salvation by offering far more than the Law required?
   b. In order to be saved must a person repent?
   c. How was your life transformed when you became a believer?

4. Luke 19:9.
   a. What do you think the Jewish onlookers thought when Jesus called the "chief tax collector" a "son of Abraham"?
   b. Galatians 3:6–7. All Jews are biological descendants of Abraham, but who does Paul identify as the true children of Abraham?

5. Luke 19:10.

   L. M. Peterson said that the story of Zacchaeus will always be remembered. "Here great opposites met, the chief of sinners and the Chief of Love, and love is triumphant."* If you know a "Zacchaeus," how can you share the love of God with them?

Memory Verse: Luke 19:10

* "Zacchaeus" in Merrill C. Tenney, ed., *Zondervan Pictorial Encyclopedia of the Bible*, vol. 5 (Grand Rapids, MI: Zondervan, 1975), 1027.

31

Trials of Jesus

Jesus was not surprised by his arrest. As the Good Shepherd, he was in complete control of his destiny: "The reason my Father loves me is that I lay down my life—only to take it up again" (John 10:17). He was a voluntary sacrifice, not a victim.

When it was time to complete his mission, Jesus began his final journey to Jerusalem (Luke 9:51). After observing the traditional Passover meal with the Twelve, Jesus went to the garden of Gethsemane to pray. Judas knew the place and had previously made a deal with the chief priests to betray Jesus (Matthew 26:14–16). He identified Jesus with a kiss—the traditional sign of respect for a rabbi (Matthew 26:47–49). Jesus was arrested by a contingent of Roman soldiers and temple guards (John 18:1–12).

The chronology of Jesus' trials is complicated because each of the four Gospels record different aspects of the trials. It was night when Jesus was arrested, and he was taken to Annas, the former high priest and father-in-law of Caiaphas, the official high priest (John 18:13–24). After questioning him, Annas sent Jesus to Caiaphas, who had assembled members of the Sanhedrin at his home. Though they didn't have evidence to convict Jesus, they spit in his face and beat him with their fists (Matthew 26:57–68). At dawn the Sanhedrin assembled for a formal trial and sentencing (Mark 15:1).

After condemning Jesus, the Sanhedrin turned him over to Pilate, the Roman governor, because they apparently did not have authority for capital punishment (John 18:31). However, they also wanted Jesus executed publicly, plus they didn't want the people to blame them for his death. (Note: Acts 7 records the stoning of Stephen, so the Jews could on occasion execute Jews for religious crimes.)

On questioning Jesus, Pilate realized he was not guilty of breaking Roman law (Matthew 27:11–23). He wanted to release him, but the Jews vehemently protested. Hoping to avoid the controversy, Pilate sent Jesus to Herod Antipas, the governor of Galilee; but Jesus refused to answer his questions. Herod sent Jesus back to Pilate (Luke 23:6–12). Again after questioning Jesus, Pilate was convinced he was innocent, but again the Jews demanded his execution. Pilate succumbed to the pressure and sentenced Jesus to die by crucifixion (Luke 23:13–25).

Study Questions

1. John 18:19–24. According to Jewish law, the high priest was not permitted to question the defendant about his guilt, yet Annas attempted to question Jesus and the guards illegally abused him. At this first hearing, there seems to have been a callous disregard for justice.
   a. What do you think motivated Annas to break Jewish law?
   b. Have you ever been treated unfairly (unjustly)? How did you feel and what did you do?

2. Mark 14:53–65. A few members of the Sanhedrin met at the house of Caiaphas during the night, though it was illegal for the Sanhedrin to meet officially at night.
   a. Why did the high priest charge Jesus with blasphemy?
   b. Have you ever been in a situation where you were falsely accused? How did you feel? What did you do?

3. Luke 23:1–5.
   a. What was the nature of the charges (civil or religious) when the religious leaders brought Jesus to Pilate? Why?

   b. Why do unbelievers usually make accusations against Christians that are related to laws and rights rather than religious beliefs?

4. Matthew 27:15–26.
   a. Why did Pilate order Jesus crucified though he knew he was innocent?
   b. What are some of the current national issues where legal decisions have been made to appease public opinion rather than what is moral or ethical?

Optional

5. Isaiah 53:7–9. How do the details of Jesus' trials fulfill Isaiah's prophecy?

Memory Verse: Mark 14:62

32

Seven Last Words of Jesus

When Jesus was crucified, he spoke seven times before he gave up his spirit. Though we should value all of Jesus' words, those he said on the cross have added value because they give us insight into what mattered most to our Savior.

None of the Gospels record all of Jesus' words from the cross. To compile a complete list we must look at all four Gospels. The following list is from the New International Version (NIV).

Matthew

1. *"Eli, Eli, lema sabachthani"* (Aramaic) "My God, my God, why have you forsaken me?" (27:46).

Mark

2. 16:34. Same as Matthew.

Luke

3. "Father, forgive them, for they do not know what they are doing" (23:34).
4. "Truly I tell you, today you will be with me in paradise" (23:43).
5. "Father, into your hands I commit my spirit" (23:46).

John

6. "Woman, here is your son," and to the disciple, "Here is your mother" (19:26–27).

7. "I am thirsty" (19:28).
8. "It is finished" (19:30).

Study Questions

1. Matthew 27:46; Psalm 22:1. The abandonment of the Son by his Father is one of the great mysteries of the crucifixion. How could the Son and the Father—who are one person—be separated, and why did God abandon his Son in his hour of greatest need? See 2 Corinthians 5:21.

   Note: Jesus was judicially or legally separated from his Father, not ontologically or in his essential being!

2. Luke 23:34; Luke 17:3–4. Why is it hard to forgive people who have offended us? How does Jesus' example on the cross help you to forgive those who have offended you?

3. Luke 23:43. The word *paradise* is related to a Persian word for "garden." Why did Jesus use the imagery of a garden to encourage the repentant thief? See 2 Corinthians 12:4 and Revelation 2:7 for other references to "paradise." When and how could you use this imagery to encourage someone who is in great pain?

4. Luke 23:35, 46.
   a. What does Jesus' prayer suggest about his power and authority to control his own death? See John 19:30 and note that Jesus bowed his head before he died.
   b. John 10:17–18. How did Jesus' death fulfill what he stated in the Good Shepherd Discourse?
   c. Why is it important to know that Jesus was in complete control of his death?

5. John 19:26–27; 13:34; 1 Timothy 5:4. What can you and/or your church do to follow Jesus' example of caring for his mother?

6. Luke 19:28; 1 Peter 2:21; 4:1–3. These passages evidence that Jesus suffered the awful pain of crucifixion and was not protected because of his deity. How can suffering help us to overcome sin?

7. John 19:30. This statement is theologically loaded. *Finished* is a commercial term for the complete payment of a debt, and the verbal sense in the Greek indicates both a completed and continuing benefit. What are some of the saving benefits we have received because of Christ's sacrificial death? See Ephesians 1:7.

Memory Verse: Isaiah 53:5–6

33

Resurrection of Jesus

The resurrection is foundational to Christianity. It validates Jesus' claim that he was the Son of God and that his death on the cross was an atoning sacrifice for sin. On the other hand, if Jesus didn't conquer death, then Christianity is simply another religion that promises a better life now but offers no hope for life after death. Paul recognizes the futility of Christianity if there is no resurrection:

> And if Christ has not been raised, our preaching is useless and so is your faith. . . . And if Christ has not been raised, your faith is futile; you are still in your sins. Then those also who have fallen asleep in Christ are lost. If only for this life we have hope in Christ, we are of all people most to be pitied.
>
> 1 Corinthians 15:14, 17–19

Paul's point is obvious. If there is no resurrection we are religious frauds and should be pitied, not admired.

Critics of course deny the resurrection and have proposed rationalistic theories to explain the empty tomb. But many of the skeptics who have tried to debunk the resurrection have become believers. Frank Morison, one of the most well known, tells of his journey of faith in the book *Who Moved the Stone?*

Study Questions

While it is impossible to prove the resurrection with absolute certainty, the New Testament gives sufficient historical evidence that Jesus rose from the dead. I have organized the evidence in the following five categories:

Scriptural—The resurrection was anticipated in the Old Testament.

1. Luke 24:25–27, 44–45. What did Jesus explain to the two men on the road to Emmaus and the disciples in the upper room?

2. Acts 2:25–32. What Old Testament prophecy did Peter quote? Why did Peter say David couldn't have been writing about himself?

3. 1 Corinthians 15:3–9. In addition to eyewitnesses, what evidence does Paul give for the resurrection?

Circumstantial—The empty tomb does not prove the resurrection but requires an explanation.

4. John 19:31–41. How would you answer the critic who says that Jesus only passed out on the cross and later regained consciousness in the tomb and escaped?

5. John 20:1–10. Why is it improbable that Mary and then Peter and John went to the wrong tomb?

6. Matthew 28:11–15. Why did the religious leaders bribe the guards to say the disciples stole the body?

Personal—Jesus appeared to numerous witnesses in varied circumstances.

7. Matthew 28:1–10. Why is it unlikely the early church would have made up stories making women the first witnesses of the resurrection?

8. 1 Corinthians 15:3–9. Does the evidence support the claim that the witnesses were emotionally unstable and experienced delusions that Jesus was alive? Why or why not?

9. John 20:26–29. What is important about Thomas's confession, "My Lord and my God"?

Historical—It is impossible to explain the birth and growth of the church apart from the resurrection. When Jesus was arrested, the disciples fled in fear. Yet, after they discovered that Jesus was alive, they could not be silenced by threats and persecution.

10. Acts 5:29–32. How would you explain the remarkable courage of the disciples if they were lying about the resurrection?

11. Acts 9:1–9. What happened to Paul on the Damascus road that convinced him to become an apostle?

Doctrinal—The resurrection is indispensable for our regeneration, justification, and glorification.

12. 1 Peter 1:3. What is the basis for our "living hope"?

13. Romans 4:25. How does the resurrection assure us that we have been justified?

14. 2 Corinthians 4:14. What will God one day do for us?

Memory Verse: Acts 2:32–33

PART 2

Acts

34

Holy Spirit and the Birth of the Church

ACTS

In the book of Acts, the function of the gift of the Spirit is different than in the Epistles, and for this reason it is provided as a separate study. In Acts the Spirit is given for power to witness and to show divine approval for the birth and growth of the church across ethnic barriers and geographical boundaries.

The church was born on the Day of Pentecost when Jesus' followers were filled with the Spirit and spoke in tongues (other languages). Peter preached a powerful message, and thousands believed, received the Spirit, and were added to the church (Acts 2:1–41). The first believers were Jews who were courageous and passionate about proclaiming the gospel but did not fully understand God's universal mission. In order to show unity between Jewish believers and different, and often despised, ethnic groups, the Pentecost event was repeated three more times in Acts. To show unity with Jewish believers, the Samaritans did not receive the Holy Spirit when they believed; rather they received the Spirit when Peter and John came from Jerusalem, prayed, and placed hands on them (Acts 8:14–17). Because of the parallels to events in Jerusalem, the conversion of Cornelius and his family has been described as the Gentile Day of Pentecost (Acts 10:44–48). When the Jerusalem church questioned Peter about the conversion of Gentiles, he answered that it was obviously a work of God because the Gentiles had received the Holy Spirit (Acts 11:15–18). The third event that parallels Pentecost is Paul's encounter with the disciples of John the Baptist. Like Peter, he laid hands on John's disciples, and they were filled with the Spirit and spoke in tongues (Acts 19:1–7). These four events are unique and intended to confirm that the ethnic and geographical growth of the church was by divine design. There are no other accounts of new believers receiving the Spirit in Acts, though they undoubtedly did.

The Spirit also provided the motivation and direction for the church's universal witness. The Holy Spirit directed the church at Antioch to anoint Paul and Barnabas for the first missionary journey (Acts 13:1–3). The Spirit prevented Paul from preaching in Asia Minor on the second journey (Acts 16:6–19). The Spirit warned Paul and his disciples about the danger of his going to Jerusalem (Acts 20:22–24; 21:1–16).

Study Questions

1. Acts 2:1–21. Peter explained to his Jewish countrymen that the giving of the Spirit at Pentecost fulfilled what had been predicted by the prophet Joel. How did the gift of the Spirit on the day of Pentecost differ from the gift of the Spirit only on certain individuals in the Old Testament?
2. Acts 2:38–41. To become a believer, what does Peter say people must do, and what does he promise God will do?
3. Acts 8:18–19. What was wrong with Simon's request to buy the power of the Holy Spirit? What are some of the ways people misunderstand and misuse the gift of the Spirit today?
4. Acts 11:15–18. How does the gift of the Spirit bring unity between people in the church who are different? How can you promote unity in your church?
5. Acts 16:6–8. What are some of the experiences in your life where you sensed that the Spirit was leading you through unexpected circumstances?

6. Acts 20:22–24. What do you think Paul meant when he said, "I am bound by the Spirit" (NLT)?
   a. Do you think the Holy Spirit leads as clearly and powerfully in our lives today as he did in Paul's? Why or why not?
   b. Have you ever felt led of the Spirit to put yourself at risk in serving Christ?
7. Why do you think Luke only recorded the gift of the Spirit to Jews, Samaritans, Gentiles, and the disciples of John the Baptist? Do you think God intended for these events to be repeated today?

Memory Verse: Acts 11:15–18

35

Baptism of Believers

Baptism, like the Lord's Supper, is a church ordinance or sacrament. John the Baptist practiced baptism as one aspect of his mission to prepare Israel for the coming of the Messiah (Matthew 3:4–6; Mark 1:4–8; Luke 3:7–9; John 1:26–28). Even Jesus was baptized by John, though his baptism was not an exact model for believer's baptism (Matthew 3:13–17; Mark 1:9–11; Luke 3:21–22; John 1:32–34). Jesus commanded baptism in the Great Commission: "Therefore go and make disciples of all nations, baptizing them in the name of the Father and of the Son and of the Holy Spirit" (Matthew 28:19).

The book of Acts contains multiple accounts of the baptism of new converts. When Peter preached on the day of Pentecost, he challenged Jews to repent and be baptized (2:38). The Samaritans were baptized (8:12), and later Cornelius and his family (Gentiles) were baptized (10:48). Lydia and her household and the Philippian jailer and his household were baptized (16:15, 33). Paul baptized the disciples of John the Baptist in the name of the Lord Jesus Christ (19:5). Paul testified about his conversion experience and baptism (22:16). Paul and all on his ship were baptized—the centurion ordered those who could swim to jump overboard first and then told the others to get to shore on planks (27:43–44). (That was a joke to see if you're paying attention!)

Two passages give the symbolic significance of baptism. In Romans 6:1–4, Paul says that we are identified with Christ in his death, burial, and resurrection. The same symbolism is found in Colossians 2:12: "having been buried with him in baptism, in which you were also raised with him through your faith in the working of God, who raised him from the dead."

In the questions, I will raise three related issues: 1) baptismal regeneration, 2) infant baptism (paedobaptism), and 3) the mode of baptism (sprinkling or immersion). One quick comment on baptismal regeneration: Though the Roman Catholic Church and some Protestant churches believe that baptism is a sacrament and essential for salvation, I do not believe the New Testament supports that view.

Study Questions

Baptismal Regeneration (Is baptism essential for salvation?)

1. 1 Corinthians 1:13–17. Does Paul's statement about his ministry in Corinth support baptismal regeneration? Why or why not?

2. Acts 10:44–48. What is the order of events in the conversion experience of Cornelius and his family? What does this suggest about the purpose of baptism?

3. Acts 22:16. Those who believe in baptismal regeneration will use this verse to support their view; however, "calling on his name" is a participial phrase indicating the action had already occurred. If this view is accepted, Paul had believed before he was baptized. What then does the verse teach about the symbolic significance of baptism?

4. Romans 6:3–4. In addition to cleansing from sins (above), what else is symbolized by baptism?

Infant Baptism (Should infants be baptized?)

5. Acts 18:7–8, 19:1–5; Titus 3:5–7. Those who advocate infant baptism believe that baptism assures that unbelieving infants will eventually become believers. What do these verses teach about the relation of faith and baptism?

The Mode of Baptism (Sprinkling or immersion?)

6. Acts 8:38–39. How was the eunuch most likely baptized?

7. Romans 6:1–4. Does the mode of baptism affect the symbolism? How?

Optional: Household Baptism

Some passages in the New Testament describe the conversion of entire households.

8. Acts 16:32–33; 16:14–15; 1 Corinthians 1:16. In addition to the jailer, who else heard the gospel? In Acts 16:40, how does Luke describe the members of Lydia's household?

Memory Verse: Romans 6:3–4

Last Words of Stephen

Stephen was the first Christian martyr. He was falsely accused of blasphemy and forced to defend himself before the Sanhedrin. Instead of defending himself, Stephen accused his Jewish countrymen of murdering the Messiah. When he finished his indictment, the Sanhedrin erupted in anger, dragged him outside the city, and stoned him (Acts 6:8–7:60).

Luke, the author of the book of Acts, has framed the account of Stephen's death so that it resembles the death of Christ. Like Christ, who spoke his last words from the cross, Stephen continued his witness and prayed for his executioners before he died.

His last words are theologically significant and practical. They give us insight into the position and ministry of Christ in heaven, how Christians should view death, and the power of forgiveness.

Study Questions

1. Acts 7:55. Why couldn't the Sanhedrin intimidate Stephen? How does this fulfill Jesus' promise in John 15:26–27? How has the Spirit given you courage when you have been in dangerous/difficult circumstances?

The following questions are related to the Christology (doctrine of Christ).

2. Acts 7:55–56.
    a. What did Stephen see when he looked into heaven?
    b. What position did Jesus assume after the exaltation (Psalm 110:1; Romans 8:34; Hebrews 1:3, 13; 10:12)? Why was Jesus standing?

Note: The right hand of God is a place of honor and authority. The Sanhedrin exploded in anger because Stephen claimed that he saw Jesus in the highest place of authority. Jesus' standing could either be interpreted in a pastoral or judicial sense. What is the implication of each?

Hint: If pastoral, what is the implication for believers at death? If judicial, does it matter if others, even Satan, are witnesses against us? Who was present as a witness against Stephen (see 8:1)? How is it encouraging to know that Jesus is our witness (see also Matthew 10:32–33; Luke 12:8)?

c. How does Stephen identify Jesus?

Note: This is the last time "Son of Man" is used in the New Testament and the only time it is used by anyone other than the Lord himself. Stephen's statement proves that Jesus is the Messiah and has been given universal authority. Jesus once again rules over all creation (cf. Ephesians 1:19–23).

d. What is the implication when Stephen sees "heaven open"? In contrast to the Levitical priests, where does Christ minister (see Hebrews 8:1–2)? Why do we now have access to the throne of God (see Hebrews 12:22–24)?

The following questions are pastoral:

3. Acts 7:59; John 19:30; Luke 23:43; Philippians 3:20–21. Before he died, Stephen prayed, "Lord Jesus, receive my spirit." Was Stephen's prayer because of uncertainty or of confidence about his eternal destination? How does this account of Stephen's death help relieve the fear of death?

4. Acts 7:60; Luke 23:34. Do you think God answered Stephen's prayer for forgiveness of his executioners? Why is

it difficult but important that we pray for our enemies? Is there someone you need to forgive? Will you pray for them?

5. Acts 22:19–20. Stephen's death apparently influenced Paul to become a believer. How do you think the way Stephen died forced Paul to reevaluate what he believed about Christ and his followers?

Memory Verse: Acts 7:56

37

Philip and the Ethiopian Eunuch

The story of the Ethiopian eunuch should not be underestimated in Luke's account of the remarkable growth of the church. The Jerusalem church was made up entirely of Jews. But Jesus had commanded his followers to make disciples of all nations (Matthew 28:18–20), so the infant church needed to expand geographically and ethnically.

Philip was one of the seven men chosen to oversee the equitable distribution of food to Greek-speaking widows in the Jerusalem church. From their names we know Philip and the other six men were Hellenists (Greek-speaking Jews) (Acts 6:5–6). As a Hellenistic Jew, Philip would have been more open-minded in witnessing to other ethnic groups.

The enemies of the church hoped to stop its rapid growth by scattering believers; instead persecution helped advance the church. When believers were forced to flee Jerusalem, Philip went to Samaria, an ethnically diverse area (Acts 8:4–5). His ministry was surprisingly successful. Many men and women believed and were baptized (Acts 8:12). The conversion of the Samaritans, who were despised by pious Jews, was a major development in the ethnic growth and geographical advance of the church.

An angel directed Philip to leave Samaria and travel south (Acts 8:26). On the road to Gaza, Philip met a treasury official from Ethiopia who had been in Jerusalem for one of the Jewish festivals; so the official was undoubtedly a convert to Judaism (Acts 8:27–28). When the Spirit directed Philip to the man's chariot, the eunuch asked Philip to explain a passage from Isaiah 53. Philip told him that the prophet was writing about Jesus (Acts 8:29–35). The Ethiopian believed and was baptized (Acts 8:36–38).

After he baptized the official, Philip was either transported by the Spirit of the Lord or guided north to Azotus; and then he went to Caesarea (Acts 8:39–40).

Why is this story important? First, though the official was most likely a convert to Judaism, he was a Gentile; so his conversion represents the crossing of a racial barrier. Second, his conversion is an advance of Christianity geographically. Third, references to an angel and the Spirit of the Lord confirm that this kind of ethnic and geographical growth was divinely directed. Fourth, Philip is a model of an obedient and faithful witness.

Study Questions

1. Acts 8:26, 29.
   a. Though angels were prominent in the growth of the early church, how does God communicate his will today?
   b. How willing are you to obey if God leads you to do something unusual?
2. Acts 8:27–28. How do you distinguish between an experience that is a divine appointment and chance?
3. Acts 8:30–35. The passage was one of the Servant Songs from Isaiah, and as Philip explained, it was a prophecy about Jesus and his suffering.
   a. Why should we include the Old Testament in our reading and study of God's word?
   b. What lessons can we learn from Philip about sharing the "good news" with others?
4. Acts 8:36, 12; 2:38, 41; Matthew 28:18–20. Though baptism does not save a person, why is it an important part of the conversion experience?

5. Acts 8:39; Philippians 4:4; Romans 14:17. Why should we be joyful rather than grumpy? How do you develop and maintain a joyful spirit in all circumstances?

Optional

6. Acts 8:27; Deuteronomy 23:1; Isaiah 56:3–8; Luke 22:20. How is the conversion of the eunuch evidence of the New Covenant?

Memory Verse: Galatians 3:28

38

Antioch

When I tell people I grew up in Yuma, most ask, "Where's that?" I tell them it's in the southwest corner of Arizona on the Colorado River. When I told my wife I was going to write on Antioch, she asked, "Where's that?" I said it was in northern Syria on the Orontes River. That didn't help much because she had never heard of the Orontes River, so I explained that I was going to write about Antioch because it was important in the advance of Christianity.

Antioch was the third largest city in the Roman Empire and a major commercial center for trade from the east, but also a cesspool of immorality. Juvenal, a Roman satirist, complained about the moral filth of Antioch when he wrote, "The sewage of the Syrian Orontes has for long been discharged into the Tiber."* What Juvenal meant was that the moral filth of Antioch polluted Rome more than 1,300 miles away.

Antioch was founded by Antiochus I. It grew in size and became prominent under the rule of Antiochus Epiphanes ("the manifest one"), known for his ruthless persecution of Jews. The city came under the control of Rome when Pompey conquered Israel and all of Syria in 63–64 BC. Though the city was occupied briefly by the Parthians, the Romans regained control and made Antioch the capital of the province of Syria. During the Roman period, Herod the Great, the appointed king of the Jews, expanded Antioch and enhanced its beauty with marble streets.

Antioch was important for the development of a multi-ethnic church. After the martyrdom of Stephen, persecution forced believers to flee Jerusalem. Some traveled as far as Antioch, ignoring

* Stanley Toussaint, "Acts," in *The Bible Knowledge Commentary*, eds. John F. Walvoord and Roy B. Zuck (Wheaton, IL: Victor Books, 1983), 383.

cultural boundaries to preach to Greeks, and a great number of Gentiles believed (Acts 11:19–21). When the Jerusalem church heard about the faith of the Gentiles, they sent Barnabas to find out what had happened (Acts 11:22–24). Barnabas recruited Paul, and both taught for a year in Antioch. It was at Antioch that believers were first called Christians (Acts 11:25–26). The church at Antioch became the sending church for Paul's three missionary journeys (Acts 13:1–3; 14:26–28; 18:22).

1. Acts 11:20–21. Why do you think some believers were motivated to preach the gospel to Gentiles but others apparently were not? What is the mind-set that motivates some believers to cross geographical and cultural boundaries to minister to people who are different?
2. Acts 11:22–24. Barnabas means "son of encouragement" (Acts 4:36). He was Jewish, the converts at Antioch Gentiles. How did he live up to his name in his response to these new believers? How would you have responded?
3. Acts 11:24. How does Luke describe Barnabas? How would Luke describe you?
4. Acts 11:26. The word *Christian* is a combination of "Christ" and "-ian," which means "belonging to the party of." It may have originally been used to ridicule believers, but believers didn't try to hide their identity. They were proud to be known as followers of Christ. How do you feel when you are publicly identified as a Christian?
5. Acts 11:27–30. What happened to help establish Antioch as a sending church?
6. Acts 13:1–3; 14:26–28. The church in Jerusalem was Jewish, the church in Antioch Gentile. Why did God lead the church in Antioch to send out the first missionaries? How is your church uniquely prepared for ministry?

Significant Passage: Acts 11:26

Barnabas

"AN ENCOURAGER"

Barnabas played a crucial role in the growth of the early church but is often overlooked because he is hidden in the shadow of the apostle Paul.

Barnabas emerges as a respected leader early in the story of the Jerusalem church. His given name was Joseph, but he was nicknamed Barnabas ("son of encouragement"). He was a Levite from Cyprus (Acts 4:37). When the poor needed help, Barnabas and other affluent members voluntarily sold land to meet their needs (Acts 4:34, 37).

We see three events in Acts that are evidence that Barnabas was indeed a "son of encouragement." He commends Paul to the apostles in Jerusalem, who were suspicious of Paul's conversion experience (Acts 9:26–27). The Jerusalem church sent Barnabas to Antioch to investigate the conversion of Gentiles. Unlike many Jewish Christians who resented Gentile converts, Barnabas was grateful because he could see that this was of God. Though Paul was a new convert, Barnabas recognized his potential and recruited him to help with a teaching ministry at Antioch (Acts 11:22–26). When the two men began discussing a second missionary journey, they got into a heated argument about John Mark, who had deserted them on the first journey. The two, who had been soul mates, separated. Paul organized a new missionary team, and Barnabas took Mark to Cyprus (Acts 15:36–41). Barnabas was successful in helping Mark to become effective in ministry (2 Timothy 4:11).

The church at Antioch commissioned Paul and Barnabas for the first missionary journey (Acts 13:1–3). At Lystra, the superstitious natives attempted to worship Barnabas and Paul as gods. They thought Barnabas was Zeus, the head of the gods, and Paul was Hermes, the spokesman for the gods (Acts 14:12).

The church at Antioch sent both Paul and Barnabas to the Jerusalem Council to resolve the conflict over Gentiles and the Law (Acts 15:1–5). In the account of the meeting Barnabas is listed first, so it is probable that he was the primary spokesman (Acts 15:12).

No one is perfect, and though an outstanding example of a devoted follower of Christ, Barnabas was led astray by Peter and discriminated against Gentiles, for which Paul reprimanded Peter (Galatians 2:11–14).

Study Questions

1. Acts 4:34–37. How can you be an encourager to someone in need?
2. Acts 11:23. Though many Jews refused to accept Gentiles into the church, Barnabas was thankful for their conversion and ministered to them. What can the church do to make new converts feel welcome and help them to know what it means to be a Christ follower?
3. Acts 11:25–26. Barnabas recognized Paul's potential for serving Christ and made a special effort to involve him in the ministry at Antioch. Is there someone you can mentor to help them realize their full potential for serving Christ?
4. Acts 15:36–41.
   a. Why do you think Barnabas was willing to give John Mark a second chance and Paul wasn't?
   b. Luke doesn't say who was right or wrong, so I don't think we should make a judgment about the two men. Rather, I think the passage reveals two different personality types. Paul was task oriented, and Barnabas people oriented. Which type are you, and what are the strengths and weaknesses of each type?

5. The world and the church need more men and women like Barnabas. How can you change the way you relate to people so you become "a son [daughter] of encouragement"?

Memory Verse: 1 Thessalonians 5:11

40

Jerusalem Council

LAW VERSUS GRACE

After Paul and Barnabas completed their first missionary journey, a group of Jewish Christians, commonly called Judaizers, attempted to force Gentiles to undergo circumcision for acceptance into the church. Circumcision was the physical sign given to Abraham to identify his descendants as God's covenant people (Genesis 17). It became the primary marker of adherence to the law of Moses for the Jewish people.

When Paul and Barnabas discovered the Judaizers were teaching Gentiles that circumcision was necessary for salvation, they went to Jerusalem to defend the gospel. The meeting known as the Jerusalem Council decided in favor of the gospel of grace and against requiring Gentiles to submit to the law of Moses (Acts 15:1–29).

Study Questions

1. Acts 15:1–4; 1 Corinthians 7:19. Though circumcision (the keeping of the Law) was a major issue in the early church, it is not an issue today. What are some of the issues confronting the church today?

2. Galatians 1:6–9. Why did Paul sternly condemn his opponents (Judaizers)? What is the problem if someone teaches a different gospel?

3. Acts 15:6–11. What was Peter's conclusion about the nature of salvation for both Jews and Gentiles (see v. 11)? Do you think that salvation is different for different groups of people today? Why or why not?

4. Acts 15:13–18. What was James's argument against requiring Gentiles to submit to the law of Moses? What are some of the barriers that we impose on people that make it difficult for them to trust Christ as Savior or join the church?

5. 1 Timothy 1:8–11. Though the Law is not essential for salvation and believers are not required to fully observe the law of Moses, how is the Law useful? What authority do you use as a guide for your lifestyle?

6. Acts 15:19–21. Though some have argued these stipulations are related to the law of Moses, the better view is that they are moral restrictions related to a Gentile lifestyle that were particularly offensive to Jewish believers. James, then, is not imposing the law of Moses on Gentiles in a different form but making a recommendation to preserve the unity of the church.
   a. What lifestyle practices are a divisive issue among believers today?
   b. What are the lessons we can learn from the Jerusalem Council for resolving conflict in the church?

Memory Verse: Acts 15:11

41

Paul's Missionary Journeys

At his conversion, Paul was appointed as "the apostle to the Gentiles" (Romans 11:13; see Acts 9:16). He became the single most important individual in the spread of Christianity throughout the Roman Empire. Though Paul served 2,000 years ago in a vastly different world, we can discern numerous practical principles for ministry from his three missionary journeys recorded in the book of Acts.

First, and perhaps most important, is that Paul and his companions were led by the Holy Spirit. When Paul and Barnabas were ministering in the church at Antioch, the Holy Spirit prompted the church to "set apart" Paul and Barnabas for the first missionary journey (Acts 13:1–3). On the second journey, the Holy Spirit prevented Paul and his companions from entering the region of Bithynia (modern-day Turkey) and directed them to Troas. There Paul saw in a vision a man of Macedonia begging him, "Come over to Macedonia and help us" (Acts 16:6–10). Paul testified to the Ephesian elders that he was "compelled by the Spirit" to preach the gospel though repeatedly warned of danger (Acts 20:22–24).

Second, Paul contextualized his message for different audiences though he always preached the gospel "that Christ died for our sins . . . that he was buried, that he was raised on the third day according to the Scriptures" (1 Corinthians 15:3–4). When Paul spoke to Jews in the synagogue at Antioch, in Pisidia, he appealed to the promises of God in Scripture (Acts 13:16–41). At Lystra, Paul tried to convince Gentiles to turn from the idols to the living God by telling of God's providential care for all nations (Acts 14:14–18). And Paul used a philosophical approach when he reasoned with the Epicurean and Stoic philosophers at Athens (Acts 17:16–34). To proclaim the "good news" to different cultural audiences, Paul used Scripture, providence, and philosophy.

Third, though Paul was a Jew and formerly a Pharisee, he preached the gospel to everyone without prejudice and seized every opportunity to tell people about Christ. We see a classic example of the diversity of Paul's ministry at Philippi. He went initially to a place of prayer because there wasn't a synagogue and ignored Jewish cultural restrictions by speaking to a group of godly women (Acts 16:11–15). He delivered a young girl from demon possession (Acts 16:16–21). He also witnessed to a Gentile. He and Silas were arrested and thrown into prison. When an earthquake broke open the prison, the jailer was going to kill himself because he thought all the prisoners had escaped. Paul stopped him and assured him that none of the prisoners had fled. Though terribly confused, the jailer released Paul and Silas and asked, "Sirs, what must I do to be saved?" Paul's answer was simple and concise, "Believe in the Lord Jesus Christ, and you will be saved . . ." The jailer dressed the men's wounds and took them to his house (Acts 16:25–33). Paul again ignored Jewish law by staying at the home of the jailer, who was a Gentile (Acts 16:34–35).

We see another aspect of Paul's diversity in ministry on his second missionary journey. In Athens he ministered to the educated elite. When he arrived in the city, Paul was deeply grieved by the rampant idolatry. But instead of leaving in disgust, he used one of the idols as an introduction for his message and tried to present the gospel to the skeptical philosophers (Acts 17:16–34).

Study Questions

1. Matthew 28:16–20. What is the extent of Jesus' command to make disciples? Is there anything in your life that prejudices you from taking the Great Commission seriously?

2. John 3:16. Who does God love? Is there anyone God does not love? Who are some of the people who are difficult to love? Why?

3. Genesis 12:1–3. In what is perhaps the first specific revelation of God's universal plan of salvation, what is the third promise to Abraham? How did God fulfill this promise? (See Matthew 1:1—who is the descendant of Abraham?)

4. Luke 4:16–20. Was Jesus' mission exclusive or inclusive? Why do we sometimes find it difficult to reach out to people who are different?

5. Acts 17:22–23. What was Paul's point of contact with the Athenian philosophers? As you think about people you know, what are some of the points of contact you could use to share the gospel?

6. Acts 13:49–52. What did Paul and Barnabas do because of opposition at Antioch? Do you think there is a point when we should stop sharing the gospel with people? When?

7. Acts 14:26–28. What did Paul and Barnabas do after they completed their first missionary journey? What is the principle?

8. Acts 14:21–25. Before returning to Antioch, Paul and Barnabas revisited the churches they had started on the first journey. What did they do, and what is the principle?

9. Acts 18:18–22. What did Paul tell the Ephesians when they asked him to spend more time with them? What is the lesson for us when we make plans for the future?

10. Acts 20:13–38. This passage records Paul's message to the Ephesian elders, the only recorded message to believers. What does Paul stress in verses 33–35, and how important is integrity in ministry (in the Christian life)?

Memory Verse: Acts 9:15–16

Peter and Paul—Two Apostles

ACTS

The book of Acts was written by Luke as a continuation of his story of Christ and the church. In addition to telling the story of the birth and growth of the church, Luke had several other purposes. We could call these subplots. One was to validate Paul as an apostle. Paul was not one of the Twelve. When we first meet him he is a fanatical persecutor of Christians, so even after his miraculous conversion on the road to Damascus, the church was suspicious of his claims and his teaching. Plus, Paul made enemies because he insisted that salvation was by faith and not works of the Law and that God's plan of redemption included Gentiles. His opponents constantly tried to undermine his apostolic authority to subvert his teaching. Luke employs a literary device that was common in Greek writing as evidence of Paul's apostleship. He compares Paul to Peter, who was one of the Twelve and was unquestionably recognized as an apostle. By showing that God worked in Paul's ministry in the same way as in Peter's, Luke shows that Paul's apostleship was divinely approved. There are approximately fifteen parallels between Peter and Paul in Acts. Most are in their actions, but some are in their messages.

The parallels are not only evidence of Paul's apostleship, but they also give us insight into how God can work through different people to accomplish his divine purposes. Though we are not Peter or Paul, we can be confident that God will use us as he did these two pillars of the early church.

Note: Luke uses the same device in his Gospel. He compares Jesus to John the Baptist to prove that, like John, Jesus was a man of God.

Study Questions

For this study, I have placed the comparisons in a chart. The first part of the study is to identify the comparisons; the second is to answer the application questions.

Parallel Actions

Peter	Paul
3:1–11	14:8–10
5:12–16	19:11–12
5:17–20	16:25–28
5:17	13:45
8:14–17	19:5–7
8:18–25	13:9–12
10:9–20	16:6–10
9:36–41	20:9–12
4:8–12	22:30–23:1

Parallels in Preaching—
Note the similar references in their messages to Jews

Peter	Paul
2:22–36	13:16–41

Questions

1. Acts 4:8–12; 23:1–3. How does the example of Peter and Paul encourage you to defend your faith in a hostile world?
2. Acts 10:9–16; 16:6–10. Though God led Peter and Paul through visions, how does God guide today? How can you help advance the kingdom by ministry to a "Cornelius" or a "man of Macedonia," to someone out of your comfort zone?
3. Peter and Paul were both Jews, but they were different. Peter was a Hebraic Jew and highly resistant to Greek and Roman culture. Paul was a Grecian Jew and more open to

Greek and Roman thinking and customs. Peter was a recognized leader in the early church, so God used him to open the door of faith to Gentiles (the conversion of Cornelius, Acts 10). But God sent Paul rather than Peter through that door because he was willing and eager to minister to Gentiles. How has God uniquely prepared you for a special ministry to others?

Memory Verse: Galatians 2:7–8

43

Sadducees

When Peter and John began teaching about the resurrection, the Sadducees were outraged. In contrast to the Pharisees, the Sadducees didn't believe in the resurrection. They ordered the temple guards to arrest the two men. They questioned them and warned them to stop teaching nonsense about the resurrection (Acts 4:1–22).

The Sadducees were a smaller religious party than the Pharisees but were influential because they controlled the office of high priest and worship in the temple. Like the Pharisees, the Sadducees are not mentioned in the Old Testament. They first appeared along with the Pharisees during the time of John Hyrcanus, a Jewish ruler from 135 to 104 BC. They were wealthy, adopted Greek customs, and supported Roman rule during the time of Christ. They were not popular with the people, lived for this life only, and did not believe in the resurrection or angels. They rejected the traditions of the Pharisees and their rigid lifestyle. Unlike the favorable comments about the Pharisee Nicodemus, there are no positive references to the Sadducees in the Gospels or Acts.

Study Questions

1. Matthew 16:5–6. The "yeast of the Pharisees and Sadducees" refers to their teachings. What teachings would Jesus warn us about today?

2. Acts 4:1–4. The primary opposition to the early church came from the Sadducees not the Pharisees. Why did the Sadducees oppose Peter and John? Why is it so difficult for people to believe in a resurrection?

3. Matthew 22:23–33. The Sadducees tried to discredit Jesus with a question about the resurrection that they thought he could not answer. How did Jesus answer? What evidence for the resurrection would you give people today?
4. Acts 2:22–31. What evidence did Peter give for the resurrection? Since the Sadducees didn't believe in the resurrection, how would they explain the empty tomb?
5. Acts 5:17–18.
   a. In addition to the apostles' teaching about the resurrection, why did the Sadducees order the apostles be arrested?
   b. What causes jealousy, and why is it so destructive?
   c. What are some ways to overcome jealousy?
6. Acts 5:19–20.
   a. How did God release the apostles?
   b. What is ironic and somewhat humorous about how the apostles were released? Remember what the Sadducees did not believe.
   c. Do you think Luke (God, the ultimate author) has a sense of humor?
7. Acts 23:6–11. Knowing that he probably would not get a fair hearing before the Sanhedrin (the Jewish supreme court), how did Paul start a violent argument between the Pharisees and Sadducees? What are some of the issues that divide Christians today?

Memory Verse: Acts 23:8

44

Samaritans

Jesus was not politically correct. He often said things that made people mad. He once told a story about a priest, a temple worker (a Levite), and a Samaritan. In contrast to the priest and the Levite, who ignored a man who had been mugged, the Samaritan helped him and even paid an innkeeper to take care of the man until he recovered (Luke 10:29–35). Most Jews despised Samaritans and would have been terribly offended by Jesus reversing the roles of the Samaritan and the priest and the Levite.

The hostility between Jews and Samaritans was centuries old. When the Assyrians conquered the Northern Kingdom (called Israel) in 722 BC, they deported most of the Jews and repopulated the area with ethnic groups from other areas of their empire. The remaining Jews eventually married non-Jews. Their descendants were called Samaritans, after Samaria, the former capital of the Northern Kingdom. The foreigners who tried to join the Jews in rebuilding the temple after the exile but were rejected by Zerubbabel were probably Samaritans (Ezra 4:1–5). In the period between the testaments, John Hyrcanus, a Jewish ruler, fought with the Samaritans and destroyed their temple on Mount Gerizim.

Jesus not only ignored ethnic differences, he ignored geographical boundaries. When traveling north from Jerusalem, he went through Samaria, which was sandwiched between the two Jewish provinces of Judea and Galilee, and stopped in the village of Sychar. He shocked an unnamed Samaritan woman by asking her for a drink and carrying on an extended conversation with her (John 4:1–42). Samaritan hostility to the Jews surfaced when Jesus wasn't allowed to enter a Samaritan village (Luke 9:51–55). Jesus' disciples were probably puzzled by his command to spread the gospel to Jerusalem, Judea, Samaria, and the ends of the earth

(Acts 1:8). When persecution forced Jesus' followers out of Jerusalem, Philip went to Samaria. Many Samaritans believed and received the Spirit by the hands of two Jewish apostles, Peter and John (Acts 8:4–25).

Study Questions

1. John 4:19–24. When the Samaritan woman asked Jesus about whether they should worship "on this mountain" or "in Jerusalem," she was referring to Mount Gerizim, where the Samaritan temple had stood.
   a. How did Jesus' answer eliminate both ethnic and geographical boundaries?
   b. What does it mean to "worship in spirit and truth" (ESV)?

2. John 4:39–42. In contrast to the majority of Jews who believed the Messiah would only save Israel, the Samaritans came to a different conclusion about Jesus. How does their conclusion affect our responsibility to share the gospel with all people?

3. Luke 9:51–55. Why was Jesus rejected by this Samaritan village? What was the reaction of James and John? How should we respond when people reject us because we are ethnically and culturally different?

4. Acts 8:4–8. From the names of the men listed in Acts 6:5, we know that Philip was culturally a Greek (Hellenistic) Jew. This means that he had undoubtedly experienced racial prejudice from Hebraic Jews and could sympathize with the Samaritans. Why would his ethnicity make it easier for him to take the good news to Samaria? How does your ethnic and/or cultural background help you to connect with people who are different?

5. Acts 8:12–17. The Samaritans didn't receive the Holy Spirit when they believed. This was not the norm. The delay was to promote the unity of Jewish and Samaritan believers by connecting the Samaritans with the Jewish church in Jerusalem through the ministry of Peter and John. (See study on the Holy Spirit.) Many believe the church in America is racially divided. Is there anything we can do to promote racial unity in the church in America?

Memory Verse: John 4:39; Acts 8:5

Three Converts at Philippi

LYDIA (PART I)

Paul's vision that called him from Troas to Macedonia resulted in the advance of Christianity geographically and culturally (Acts 16:6–10). Sailing from Troas to Neapolis took Paul from Asia to Europe, establishing Christianity on two continents. The conversions of Lydia, the slave girl, and the jailer at Philippi show the triumph of Christianity over Judaism, demonism, and paganism (Acts 16:11–40). I have divided this study into three parts to make it manageable for individuals and groups.

The Triumph of Christianity over Judaism

Lydia was the first convert to Christianity in Europe. On his second missionary journey, Paul was led by the Spirit to go from Asia to Europe. He sailed from Troas to Neapolis and then traveled on land to Philippi, a major city in the Roman province of Macedonia (Acts 16:11–12).

On the Sabbath, because there was no synagogue, Paul went to "a place of prayer" and spoke to women gathered for prayer. A businesswoman named Lydia was there. Her name suggests she was a Gentile, but she is identified as "a worshiper of God," a common designation for a convert to Judaism. She was from Thyatira, an area known for the production of purple cloth, and she was "a dealer in purple cloth." Purple was the favorite color of royalty and the rich, so cloth dyed purple was extremely expensive (Acts 16:13–14).

As Paul was speaking, the Lord "opened her heart." Lydia became a believer and was baptized. We don't know why she didn't have a husband, but because she was the head of her household, all became believers. She demonstrated that her faith was genuine by extending hospitality to Paul and his companions, and Paul accepted her hospitality though she was a Gentile (Acts 16:14–15).

Study Questions

1. Why did Paul speak to women rather than men at "a place of prayer"? What are the implications for the church's ministry to women? Should the church have ministries that are specifically for women?
2. Luke says the Lord opened Lydia's heart. How is a conversion experience a matter of both the heart and mind?
3. Lydia was successful in business, and there is no evidence she left her business after becoming a believer. How can believers maintain a healthy balance between their faith and their work?
4. Lydia, a Gentile, opened her home to Paul and his companions, Jews, as evidence of her faith. How can new believers today show that their faith is genuine?
5. Paul's willingness to stay at Lydia's home was an affirmation of her as a person of equal value. How can we affirm to new believers that they matter to God and to us?
6. Lydia and her household were baptized after they believed. Baptism doesn't save a person, but why is it an important part of the conversion process?

Memory Verse: Philippians 1:3–6

46

Three Converts at Philippi

THE SLAVE GIRL/HUMAN TRAFFICKING (PART II)

The first convert at Philippi was Lydia, a businesswoman. The second was a demon-possessed slave girl.

The Triumph of Christianity over Demonism

The girl was possessed by "a spirit of Python," *puthon* (Acts 16:16, my translation). According to the Greek legend, the mythological serpent that guarded the oracle at Delphi was killed by Apollo. "The spirit of Python," however, lived on, giving anyone it possessed the ability to predict the future. Her owners exploited the girl as a fortune-teller. The girl made a nuisance of herself by following Paul and Silas, shouting, "These men are servants of the Most High God." Paul didn't want or need the testimony of a demon-possessed girl, so speaking directly to the spirit, Paul exorcised the demon (Acts 16:16–18).

When the girl's owners realized they had lost their source of income, they seized Paul and Silas and brought them before the city officials (magistrates). They accused them of illegal practices. Rome allowed the colonies to practice their own religion, but they could not persuade others to convert. However, though the Philippians were proud of their citizenship, they violated Roman law when they beat and imprisoned Paul and Silas without a trial (Acts 16:19–24).

Though the text does not describe her conversion experience, the slave girl undoubtedly became a believer. Her conversion shows the triumph of Christianity over demonism.

Study Questions

1. Acts 16:16. Though slavery is illegal in most countries, human trafficking is a massive problem in the world. What are some of the similarities between slavery and human trafficking? How can Christians (the church) respond to human trafficking?

2. Acts 16:19; 1 Timothy 6:9–10. What is the motivation for human trafficking? What are some of the evils (sins) that result from greed? What can we do to avoid the love of money?

3. Mark 1:24; Acts 16:17. What was the demon's testimony about Jesus and his mission? What did the slave girl shout about Paul and his mission? How did Paul's ministry and how does our ministry today advance the mission of Jesus? See Colossians 1:13–14.

4. Acts 16:18; Mark 1:25, 34. Why didn't Jesus and Paul allow demons to testify about their mission? See Acts 1:8. What is our responsibility in proclaiming the gospel and why wouldn't we want the testimony of unbelievers, especially those with opposing religious beliefs?

5. Acts 16:19–21. What are some of the complaints (charges) that unbelievers make against Christians today? What kind of prejudice have you experienced and how did you respond?

6. Acts 16:22–24; Acts 9:15–16; 2 Corinthians 11:25. How did Paul's experience at Philippi fulfill what was predicted when he became a believer? Why are we reluctant to talk about suffering for Christ? Should we explain to those considering becoming a Christian that following Christ involves suffering? Why or why not?

Memory Verse: Colossians 1:13

47

Three Converts at Philippi

THE JAILER (PART III)

The first two converts at Philippi were Lydia, an affluent businesswoman, and a demon-possessed slave girl. The third was the Philippian jailer. His conversion shows the triumph of Christianity over paganism.

The jailer's encounter with Paul and Silas was by divine providence. When Paul tried to proclaim the gospel, he was constantly harassed by a demon-possessed slave girl, who was exploited by her owners for profit. Paul confronted the demon and cast it out in the name of Jesus Christ. She lost her ability to predict the future, and her owners lost money since she could no longer tell fortunes. Freeing someone from demon possession was not a crime; instead her owners accused Paul of breaking Roman law for attempting to make converts. He and Silas were not given an opportunity to defend themselves. They were beaten, thrown into a dungeon, and their feet placed in stocks (Acts 16:16–24).

Instead of grumbling and complaining, Paul and Silas prayed and sang. God used an earthquake to free the men from their chains and open the doors of the prison. The two could have easily escaped, but they didn't. When the jailer realized the prison was wide open, he planned to kill himself rather than be executed. Paul stopped him and assured the jailer no one had escaped. The frightened jailer cried out for help, "Sirs, what must I do to be saved?" (Acts 16:30). In one of the most concise statements of faith in the Bible, Paul said, "Believe in the Lord Jesus, and you will be saved—you and your household" (Acts 16:31). Though it was the middle of the night, the jailer treated their wounds, took them home, and fed them. He and his household believed and were baptized (Acts 16:25–34).

The magistrates wanted to release Paul and Silas secretly, but Paul insisted they escort them out of the prison. When the city officials found out Paul and Silas were Roman citizens, they were frightened, apologized, and personally released them. Paul's insistence that the officials personally release them was not vindictive; he wanted a public admission of the apostles' innocence. He and his companions returned to Lydia's house and encouraged the new believers before leaving for Thessalonica (Acts 16:35–40).

Study Questions

1. Acts 16:22–24; Philippians 1:12. How have unexpected circumstances in your life helped advance the kingdom of God?
2. Acts 16:25–26; Philippians 1:19. Would God have freed Paul and Silas if they hadn't prayed? To what extent do you think prayer changes our circumstances? What circumstances in your life have been changed because of prayer?
3. Acts 16:27–28.
    a. Why didn't Paul and the other prisoners escape when they had the opportunity? Did they know the jailer would be executed if they escaped?
    b. What is more important when we are in difficult or even dangerous situations, that we pray for deliverance or that we ask God how we can use those circumstances to do his will?
4. Acts 16:29–31.
    a. How did the jailer and possibly the other prisoners hear the message of salvation?
    b. What does it mean "to believe in the Lord Jesus"?

c. Acts 16:14. Why did Lydia become a believer? What is God's part and what is our responsibility in salvation?

5. Acts 16:32–34. How did the jailer show that he had become a believer? When you became a Christian, what did you do as evidence of your faith?

6. Acts 16:35–40. Paul was not vindictive in demanding the city officials personally release them; rather, he wanted public recognition that Christianity was not illegal in the Roman empire. His concern was the legal status of the new Christian movement, not his personal reputation. When should believers use their rights as citizens to advance Christianity?

Memory Verse: Acts 16:30–31

48

Trials of Paul

Paul's arrest, trials, and voyage to Rome were the direct consequence of his courageous decision to preach the gospel in Jerusalem and Rome (Acts 19:21).

When he arrived in Jerusalem at the end of his third journey, Paul reported to the Jewish church about his ministry among Gentiles. James and the elders were thankful but informed Paul of rumors that he was encouraging Jews to abandon the law of Moses. They recommended that Paul join and help pay the expenses for four men to complete a Nazirite (Jewish) vow. When Paul entered the temple area to complete the vow, Jews from Asia charged he had taken Gentiles with him into the temple. The accusation started a riot. Paul was seized, and the mob was attempting to beat him to death when the Romans intervened. They arrested Paul, thinking he was a terrorist (Acts 21:17–38).

Paul insisted he was not a terrorist and asked if he could speak to his people. Paul told them about his miraculous conversion; but when he said that God had commissioned him to go to the Gentiles, the mob exploded in anger. Convinced that Paul was trying to start a riot, the commander ordered him flogged, but Paul claimed his rights as a Roman citizen (Acts 21:39–22:29).

The Romans placed Paul under protective custody and arranged for him to speak to the full Sanhedrin. Paul knew he wouldn't get a fair hearing so he instigated a violent debate between the Pharisees and Sadducees over the resurrection (Acts 22:30–23:11).

When Paul's nephew discovered a plot to assassinate the apostle, the Romans transferred him to Caesarea (Acts 23:12–35). The high priest and Jewish elders hired a lawyer to make formal charges against Paul. Though Paul refuted the charges, Felix held him as a prisoner to appease the Jews and in hopes of a bribe. After two years, Felix was replaced by Festus (Acts 24). When King Agrippa and his sister Bernice came to pay their respects to the new governor, Paul gave his defense and testimony to all three. None became believers, but they concluded that Paul was not a criminal (Acts 25–26).

Paul had used his rights as a Roman citizen to make an appeal to Caesar, so Festus put Paul on a ship for transfer to Rome. The ship was wrecked by a violent storm, but Paul and all on board made it safely to Rome. Paul was held under house arrest until he could make his appeal to Caesar (Acts 27–28).

Study Questions

1. Acts 19:21–22; 21:10–13.
    a. Why was Paul determined to go to Jerusalem though he knew that he would be arrested?
    b. What plans or decisions have you made that seem unreasonable to others?
    c. In making decisions when should we follow the counsel of others and when should we ignore it?
2. Acts 21:37–40. How did Paul use his circumstances for an opportunity to give his testimony?
3. Acts 22:24–29. When should we use our rights as citizens to defend ourselves against civil authorities?
4. Acts 23:1–3. Do you think it was right or wrong for Paul to insult the high priest?
5. Acts 23:12–22. Do you think it was luck or divine providence that Paul's nephew found out about the plot to assassinate Paul? How do you know the difference between luck and divine providence?
6. Acts 24:24–26. Why do you think Felix was afraid? Why is it risky for people to put off a decision to receive Christ?

7. Acts 26:24–29. Both Festus and Agrippa refuted Paul's testimony. What are the reasons people today refuse to trust Christ?

Memory Verse: Acts 24:15–16

Troas

Located on the northwest coast of Asia Minor, Troas was the closest and most convenient port for anyone traveling from Asia Minor to Europe. It was a Greek city, founded during the era of Alexander the Great. After the division of his empire, the Seleucid dynasty in Syria controlled the city, but surrendered it to the Romans when Rome expanded its empire in the east.

Western Christianity owes its existence to Paul's experience at Troas. On his second missionary journey, Paul and his companions tried to go directly west to the province of Asia, but the Holy Spirit stopped them. When they turned north, the Spirit of Jesus kept them from going into the province of Bithynia. They were divinely directed to Troas, where Paul saw a vision of a man of Macedonia pleading, "Come over to Macedonia and help us." After Paul and his companions discussed the vision, they concluded God was calling them to Europe (Acts 16:6–10). Paul's ministry in Europe on his second journey would establish Christianity on two continents, Asia and Europe. Had he not responded to the vision, Christianity might have been only an eastern religion.

The book of Acts contains only two descriptions of the early church. At the end of chapter 2, Luke describes the Jewish church in Jerusalem. In chapter 20, he describes the Gentile church at Troas. We do not have any information on how a church was started at Troas, but Paul returned there on his third journey. His experience was again unusual and memorable. Luke, who was a physician, focuses on what happened to a sleepy young man who fell out of a third-story window. Paul took Eutychus in his arms and said, "Don't be alarmed. He's alive!" After speaking all night, Paul departed and never returned to Troas (Acts 20:7–12).

Study Questions

1. Acts 16:6–8. Luke does not tell us how the Holy Spirit prevented Paul and his companions from going to the provinces of Asia and Bithynia, but it was probably through circumstances. How do you respond to circumstances that force you to make major changes in your plans?
2. Acts 16:9–10. Though Paul had a vision of a man calling him to Macedonia, why do you think he discussed the decision to go to Macedonia with his companions? How do you make important decisions?
3. Acts 16:10. The decision to go to Macedonia might have seemed small to Paul and his companions, but it resulted in Christianity spanning two continents, Asia and Europe. What small decisions have you made that have had an impact far beyond what you anticipated?
4. Acts 2:42–47; 20:7–12. What are some of the similarities and differences between the Jewish church in Jerusalem and the Gentile church in Troas?
5. Acts 2:42–47; Acts 20:7–12. What are some of the features of the early church that the church today should duplicate and what are some that can't be duplicated?
6. Acts 20:7. On what day of the week did the church meet? Why? What made this day special? What would you say to a person who says the church should meet on Saturday?
7. Acts 20:7. The early church met in the evening because most of the early believers were from the working class and could only come to church in the evening after work. What is the implication of this for the day and time churches should meet?

8. Acts 20:9–12. Eutychus's name means "lucky one." Why was he lucky? What is the similar event in Acts 9:36–41? How were these events a confirmation of the ministry of these two men in new geographical areas?

Memory Verse: Acts 16:9–10

PART 3

Paul's Epistles

50

Baptism for the Dead

1 CORINTHIANS 15

I first learned about baptism for the dead when I was the pastor of a small church in the Southwest. When a family decided to join our church they asked if their daughter could be baptized. I said, "Of course!" When I talked to their daughter about baptism I was surprised to learn that she had been baptized over fifty times. She explained that she had been a member of the Mormon Church and that they practiced proxy baptism for the dead. She had been baptized for people she didn't even know.

Only one verse in the Bible mentions baptism for the dead: "Now if there is no resurrection, what will those do who are baptized for the dead? If the dead are not raised at all, why are people baptized for them?" (1 Corinthians 15:29). What is the meaning and the application of this difficult verse? One commentator has stated that there are over 200 interpretations and most attempt to relate it to baptism of the living. First, we should note that Paul frequently quotes Corinthian slogans to correct problems, not to teach church doctrine. They claimed that "everything is permissible" (1 Corinthians 6:12 CSB) to condone their sexual immorality, but Paul said unrestrained liberty is not necessarily good. Second, Paul does not encourage baptism for the dead. In fact he makes it clear that it is not his practice. He refers to "those" who are baptized for the dead, not "we." Third, it is possible that some in the church had been influenced by the mystery religions that practiced baptism for the dead.

Study Questions

1. 1 Corinthians 15:29.
   a. Why didn't Paul give us more information on baptism for the dead?
   b. What are the dangers of basing what we believe and practice on passages that we cannot clearly understand?
   c. Are there other subjects on which you wish the Bible gave us more information?
   d. What would you say to a person who belongs to a group that practices baptism for the dead?
2. Luke 16:19–31. What does the parable of the rich man and Lazarus reveal about the destiny of people after they have died?
3. Acts 17:10–12. The Bereans are often used as an example of how we should study the Bible.
   a. How did they respond to Paul's message?
   b. What should be our ultimate standard for determining whether or not a doctrine or practice is true?
4. Wayne Grudem gives the Corinthian practice as an example of how groups use obscure portions of Scripture as a basis for their doctrine and practice.* Is there anything you believe or practice that is not clearly taught in Scripture?

Memory Verse: Acts 2:38

* Wayne Grudem, *Systematic Theology* (Grand Rapids, MI: Zondervan, 1994), 134.

51

Church Leaders

Before I became a professor of Bible, I was a pastor. I actually had the privilege and challenge of starting a church under the sponsorship of another church. People in the congregation called me "Pastor." I never thought much about what that meant. I just assumed that was my title and went about the work of a pastor.

Most orthodox churches today are served by men or women called "pastors," but this is not the only term for leaders in the early church. When Paul and Barnabas retraced the route of their first missionary journey, they appointed "elders" in the churches they had previously started (Acts 14:23). In the Pastoral Epistles of 1 Timothy and Titus, Paul lists the qualifications for the position of an "elder," "bishop," or "overseer" (1 Timothy 3:1–7; Titus 1:5–9). In Ephesians 4:11, Paul identifies "pastors" and "teachers." (It is possible that the phrase refers to two functions of the same office, "pastor/teacher.") There were "prophets" and "teachers" in the church at Antioch (Acts 13:1). We have teachers in the church today but not official prophets, though some claim they are prophets.

The qualifications for elders are listed in 1 Timothy 3 and Titus 1. The two lists are not identical, but both begin with the same general qualification: "above reproach" (1 Timothy 3:2) and "blameless" (Titus 1:6). I think this is the general qualification and all the other qualifications clarify what it means to be above reproach or blameless.

When faced with a problem of providing food for needy widows, the early church selected seven men to fix the problem (Acts 6:1–7). Though they were not called "deacons," they functioned like deacons, serving the needs of the church, and are considered the prototype for deacons, who are identified in 1 Timothy 3:8–10.

Study Questions

1. Acts 14:23. The term "elder" is plural, "elders." Do you think it is a requirement that churches have more than one elder? What are the advantages and disadvantages of a plurality of elders?

2. Titus 1:6; 1 Timothy 3:2. What do you think blameless or above reproach means?

3. 1 Timothy 3:1. Why do you think Paul says, "Whoever aspires to be an overseer . . ."? Why or why not is it important that prospective elders desire the position?

4. 1 Timothy 5:17–20.
    a. What does Paul mean by "double honor"? How important is it for an elder to receive adequate compensation for their ministry?
    b. Why does Paul say it is important to "reprove" an elder if they sin?
    c. How can you honor your pastor and elders (church leaders) in your church?

5. 1 Timothy 3:1–7; Titus 1:5–9.
    a. What qualifications are the same and different in the two lists?
    b. Do you think the qualifications are absolute or is there some degree of leniency based on circumstances?
    c. One of the most controversial items in the two lists is "faithful to his wife," literally, "the husband of one wife." It has been interpreted to mean that an elder (1) must be married, (2) cannot have more than one wife (polygamy), (3) must not be divorced, or (4) cannot be remarried. An alternate view is that an elder "must be faithful to his one wife." Why do you think marital status is an important qualification for an elder?

Optional

6. Do you think these qualifications apply to the lifestyle of all Christians?

7. Do you think women can serve as elders in the church today? Why or why not?

Memory Verse: Acts 20:28–31

52

Church, Metaphors

When you hear the expression "the body of Christ," what do you think of? If you're like most believers, you think of the church because it is the most well-known way of describing the church. The New Testament writers, however, use a wide variety of metaphors or figures of speech to help us understand the nature of the church.

Paul uses the metaphor of the body in multiple ways. In 1 Corinthians 12:12–31 he emphasizes that all members of the body have received the Spirit and are equally important. He assures the Ephesians that they have nothing to fear from demonic powers because they are Christ's body, and Christ reigns with absolute authority over all powers in the universe (Ephesians 1:18–23). Paul willingly endures suffering for "the sake of his body, which is the church" (Colossians 1:24). He stresses that the church is "one body" to encourage harmony between Jews and Gentiles (Ephesians 2:14–18). To refute false teachers who had a deficient understanding of the full deity of Christ, Paul says Christ is "the head of the body, the church" and "God was pleased to have all his fullness dwell in him" (Colossians 1:18–20). Christ is also "the head," who equips his body and enables its members to grow to maturity (Ephesians 4:11–16).

Study Questions

1. In the above passages on the metaphor of "the body," which is the most helpful to you and why?

In the following passages, what is the metaphor and its purpose?

2. 1 Corinthians 3:5–17. Paul uses three metaphors.

3. 1 Peter 2:9. There are two metaphors in the passage.
4. Romans 11:16–24.
5. 1 Corinthians 6:19.
6. 1 Timothy 3:14–15. What are the two metaphors?
7. Ephesians 5:31–33; Revelation 19:6–8.
8. Which of these metaphors is the most encouraging and the most challenging? Why?

Memory Verse: Ephesians 1:22–23

53

Fruit of the Spirit

Jesus used the analogy of a vine and its branches to teach about fruitfulness (John 15:1–8). Jesus did not explain exactly what he meant by fruitfulness, only that it was necessary to "abide" or "remain" in him. Though Paul didn't quote Jesus directly, he was probably thinking of his teaching on fruitfulness when he contrasted the works of the flesh with the fruit of the Spirit (Galatians 5:19–23).

In Galatians 5 Paul explains how believers should walk in the Spirit rather than in the fleshly desires of the old life. Instead of following the impulses of the sinful nature, Paul says that we should rely on the Holy Spirit to produce the spiritual virtues of "love, joy, peace, forbearance, kindness, goodness, faithfulness, gentleness and self-control" (vv. 22–23).

"Fruit" is singular, emphasizing the harmonious unity of the virtues and that together they give a composite character portrait of what it means to be like Christ. Though anyone can possess these virtues in varying degrees, for believers they are developed by the work of the Spirit (2 Corinthians 3:18).

Study Questions

Habits of the Mind: Love, Joy, Peace

1. 1 John 4:16–21. What is the fundamental characteristic of God? What is the benefit of perfect love in the life of a believer? What is your greatest fear, and how can love help you to overcome it?

2. Philippians 1:18–19. Though Paul was a prisoner in Rome when he wrote to the Philippians, why did he rejoice? How

can we cultivate an attitude of joy when we experience difficult circumstances?

3. Philippians 4:4–7. In this passage Paul combines joy and peace. How can prayer help us to experience peace in all circumstances? What in your life do you need to commit to God in prayer?

Virtues in Relationships: Forbearance (Patience), Kindness, Goodness

4. 2 Corinthians 6:6. Patience (*makrothumia*) is "putting up" with people, especially those who are offensive, by refusing to retaliate when mistreated. Luke 23:34. How did Jesus respond to his executioners? How can we show patience toward those who mistreat us?

5. Romans 2:4. Why is God kind toward sinners? How can you show kindness to a person who is generally disliked by others?

6. 1 Thessalonians 5:15. Goodness is both an attribute and action. What does Paul exhort the Thessalonians to do for each other and "everyone else"? What specifically does it mean "to do what is good"? How can we show goodness to others?

Virtues of Character (Faithfulness, Gentleness, Self-Control)

7. Habakkuk 2:4. Faithfulness is reliability or trustworthiness. Luke 16:10–13. According to Jesus, why is it important for us to be faithful in the small matters of life? How can we keep from being distracted from our devotion to God by worldly pursuits?

8. Ephesians 4:2; 1 Peter 3:15. Gentleness is strength of character that enables us to show respect for others in all kinds

of circumstances. How can we show respect for those with whom we disagree on political or lifestyle issues?

9. Acts 24:25. Self-control is restraining the impulses of the sinful nature, something that the Roman governor Felix was unable to do. How can we control the desires of the flesh (Galatians 5:16)? What does it mean to walk by the Spirit?

Memory Verse: Galatians 5:22–23

54

Heavenlies/Heavenly Realms

"Great is Artemis of the Ephesians!" the mob shouted in protest against Paul (Acts 19:34). The city of Ephesus was dominated by the cult of Artemis. The superstitious Ephesians had built one of the most magnificent temples in the ancient world on the location where they believed the image of the goddess Artemis had fallen from heaven. Artemis was worshiped as a fertility goddess because the image was most likely a meteorite shaped like a multi-breasted woman. Pilgrims came from all over the Roman Empire to worship the goddess and buy small silver images to take home, believing that the idol would bring them prosperity.

Paul ministered in Ephesus on his third missionary journey and persuaded many who had been enslaved in the occult to turn to Christ. They repented and burned their books on magic. The conversion of so many to Christianity was a threat to the livelihood of the silversmiths who sold images of Artemis to worshipers. Demetrius, a leader of the silversmiths, organized a protest, but it quickly deteriorated into a riot. The mayor (city clerk) intervened and restored order (Acts 19).

A church was started in Ephesus; and though Paul did not return to the city, he met with the Ephesian elders on the island of Miletus (Acts 20:13–38). And later while he was under house arrest in Rome (Acts 28:30–31) he wrote a letter to the Ephesians and other churches in the area. Knowing that the Ephesian believers had been deeply immersed in the occult, Paul gives a unique perspective on the church and what it means to be "in Christ." He opens with an amazing statement, "God . . . has blessed us in the heavenly realms with every spiritual blessing in Christ" (Ephesians 1:3). The term *heavenlies* or *heavenly realms* is not a reference to heaven. It occurs five times in Ephesians (1:3, 20; 2:6; 3:10; 6:12), and refers to the spiritual realm where Christ now rules with absolute authority over all other powers. Paul states what is almost incomprehensible for us who still live in the earthly, physical realm. Because believers are spiritually united with Christ, we are also ruling over all spiritual forces in the cosmos (Ephesians 1:19–23). The Ephesians need not fear Satan and his diabolical minions; they are victors with Christ in the heavenly realms. They can look up now, not in the future, where they sit enthroned with Christ at the right hand of God. And while still on earth, they are protected by the full armor of God (Ephesians 6:10–17).

Study Questions

1. Ephesians 2:6. How does knowing that "heavenly realms" is not a reference to heaven but to our present spiritual status affect how you think about your relationship with Christ?
2. Ephesian 1:3. What spiritual blessings do we have because we are united with Christ?
3. Ephesians 1:15–23.
    a. What is Paul's prayer for the Ephesians?
    b. How does Paul describe the church?
    c. How can you use Paul's prayer to pray for others?
4. Ephesians 3:10. How does knowing that you are God's trophy on display to "the rulers and authorities in heavenly realms" make a difference in how you live?
5. Ephesians 6:10–12.
    a. Who does Paul identify as our enemy?
    b. What are some of the devil's schemes?
    c. How can we protect ourselves?
6. Ephesians 6:18–20. What is Paul's emphasis in this passage? Why is prayer important?

7. How do you think the Epistle affected the Ephesians' fears about evil spirits (demons)? Do you think Christians today have any reason to fear demons?

Memory Verse: Ephesians 2:6

55

Last Words of Paul

Karl Marx is reported to have said, "Last words are for a man who hasn't said enough during his lifetime." Karl Marx was wrong. Last words are important because they often reveal what a person valued in life, how they want to be remembered, and what they want to pass on to the next generation.

Paul was a prisoner in Rome twice. He was held under house arrest for two years and then released (Acts 28:30–31). Paul resumed his travels and ministry, but during a brief period of persecution under the emperor Nero, he was rearrested. He wrote 2 Timothy while awaiting trial. He expected to be executed rather than acquitted. To inspire Timothy and future generations of believers, Paul gave an assessment of his life and over twenty years of devoted service for his Lord and Savior.

Paul's "last words" are recorded in 2 Timothy 4:6–8.

Study Questions

1. 2 Timothy 4:6; Numbers 28:6–8. The "drink offering" was supplemental to the primary "burnt offering." Why does Paul consider his life a "drink offering"? What or who was the primary offering? In what ways do our lives supplement the sacrifice of Christ? See Colossians 1:24.

2. 2 Timothy 4:6; Philippians 1:23. "Depart" is a euphemism for die. How does viewing the end of life as a departure change your view of dying? What is our destination? (See 2 Corinthians 5:8.)

3. 2 Timothy 4:7. See also 1 Timothy 6:12 and Acts 20:24. What is the meaning of the two athletic metaphors Paul

uses in this verse? What two metaphors would you use to describe your life?

4. 2 Timothy 4:7. What does it mean to keep the faith? In the context of 1 Timothy "faith" refers to Christian truth (beliefs) rather than "saving faith" (cf. 1 Timothy 1:19–20).

   Note: I do not think Hymenaeus and Alexander lost their salvation (saving faith) but abandoned fundamental truths of the Christian faith.

5. 2 Timothy 4:8. The "crown of righteousness" was the laurel wreath awarded to victorious athletes and could mean either the righteousness that comes from faith in Christ (Philippians 3:9) or a special reward for righteousness in life and service for Christ (James 1:12; Revelation 2:10).
   a. Why was Paul unafraid to be judged by the Lord?
   b. What spiritual disciplines do you practice to help you live righteously?

6. 2 Timothy 4:8. "Day" is referring to the Lord's return, not the time of death. What do you fear will disqualify you for the crown of righteousness when the Lord returns?

7. Though it's a bit morbid, if given the opportunity, what do you hope to say about yourself at the end of your life?

Memory Verse: 2 Timothy 4:8

56

Lord's Supper

COMMUNION

The Lord's Supper, or Communion, is one of two church ordinances. The other is baptism. By ordinance we mean an event that the church has been commanded to observe. The Lord Jesus instituted the Lord's Supper at the Passover meal he observed with the Twelve before he was arrested. After taking some bread Jesus broke it, saying, "Take it; this is my body" (Mark 14:22). He then took a cup of wine and gave it to his disciples, saying, "This is my blood of the covenant, which is poured out for many. . . . I will not drink again from the fruit of the vine until that day when I drink it new in the kingdom of God" (Mark 14:23–25).

The Passover meal and the transfiguration are the only two events from the life of Christ recorded in the Epistles (1 Corinthians 11:17–33; 2 Peter 1:16–18). Like many other aspects of church life, the Corinthians had corrupted the Lord's Supper. What Paul wrote was to correct their abuses, but he has given us important information on observing the Lord's Supper.

Study Questions

1. Matthew 26:26–29. What are the two elements we take at communion?
    a. What does the bread symbolize?
    b. What did Jesus say the cup symbolizes?
2. Matthew 26:23–24. Judas was present and apparently ate bread and drank wine. Should unbelievers participate in the Lord's Supper? Why or why not?

3. Luke 22:14–18. What does Jesus' statement that he will not eat this meal again "until the kingdom of God comes" imply about the future and our reunion with Christ?

4. 1 Corinthians 11:26. What does the Lord's Supper symbolize?

5. 1 Corinthians 11:23–26. Paul does not state how often the church should celebrate the Lord's Supper. How often does your church observe Communion? Do you think your church should observe Communion more often or less? What are the advantages and disadvantages of celebrating Communion every week?

6. 1 Corinthians 11:27–30.
   a. What does Paul say we should do to prepare ourselves for Communion? How do you prepare for communion?
   b. What is the sin of eating the bread and drinking the cup "in an unworthy manner"?
   c. The reference in verse 29 to "the body of Christ" most likely means the church body. (Some believe it is the Lord's body.) Disdain for others was a major problem in the church at Corinth. How can we "discern" (honor) others in our church?

7. 1 Corinthians 11:17–22, 33–34. In these verses Paul is referring to the agape meal (love feast) at church prior to the Lord's Supper. The wealthy came early, made gluttons of themselves, and did not leave anything for the working poor who came later. What does your church do or what can it do to provide help for its poorer members?

Optional

8. 1 Corinthians 11:27–30. Paul warns that Christians who do not properly observe the Lord's Supper bring judgment on

themselves. Some in the church at Corinth apparently had become sick and even died. Will believers today become sick or die if they abuse Communion? Why or why not?

Memory Verse: 1 Corinthians 11:26

Paul's Legacy—Seven Metaphors for the Christian Life

2 TIMOTHY 2

At various times in my ministry I have been asked to describe a Christ follower. I struggled with that question until I discovered 2 Timothy 2. Second Timothy is Paul's last epistle. He was in prison for a second time, and unlike his first imprisonment, which was house arrest, he did not expect to be set free (Acts 28:30–31; 2 Timothy 4:16–18). Knowing his life on earth was soon to end, Paul's primary concern was for his legacy. He was concerned about the perpetuation of the Christian faith from generation to generation.

Paul had commissioned Timothy for ministry in Ephesus and was deeply concerned for his son in the faith. He prayed for him constantly (2 Timothy 1:3–4), assured him he had no reason to be ashamed of Christ or the gospel (2 Timothy 1:8), and urged him to follow Paul's example of faithfully teaching the truth (2 Timothy 1:13–14).

But Paul didn't want his ministry to end with Timothy. He compares Christian truth to a "good deposit," and tells Timothy to guard it (2 Timothy 1:14). Strengthened by grace, he is to teach those who are trustworthy, so they can then teach other reliable believers (2 Timothy 2:1–2). In this way the Christian faith will be passed from one generation to the next. To describe what it means to be a faithful Christ follower, Paul uses seven different metaphors in rapid succession.

Study Questions

1. 2 Timothy 2:1–2. What are the qualities of a "reliable" and "qualified" **teacher**?

2. 2 Timothy 2:3; 1:8. Like a **soldier**, what are some of the hardships you have experienced because you are a Christ follower?

3. 2 Timothy 2:4; 1:15. What are some of the worldly attractions that can distract from our devotion to Christ?

4. 2 Timothy 2:5. **Athlete.** What are some of the rules we need to obey? What is the relationship between obedience and love? (See John 15:9–10.)

5. 2 Timothy 2:6. **Farmer.** How is the Christian life like farming? (See 1 Corinthians 3:5–9.)

6. 2 Timothy 2:15. **Workman or laborer.** What is the difference between "doing" our best and "being" the best? What does doing your best mean for you?

7. 2 Timothy 2:20–21. **Sanctified vessel.** Paul's admonition is to avoid becoming contaminated (unclean) by contact with corrupt vessels so we are no longer suitable for serving Christ. How do you keep yourself from becoming corrupted by false teaching?

8. 2 Timothy 2:24–26. **Servant.** How should we respond to our opponents, especially false teachers? What should be our goal in instructing those in error?

Optional

9. 2 Timothy 2:26. What is "the trap of the devil"? How do we avoid it?

Memory Verse: 2 Timothy 2:15

58

Paul's Thorn in the Flesh

As a boy growing up in the hot, dry desert of the Southwest, I often went barefoot in the summer. My mother had to pull more than one thorn out of my bare feet. My experience wasn't the same as Paul's "thorn in the flesh," but thorns are painful.

Paul tells the Corinthians that God gave him "a thorn in [the] flesh" to keep him from becoming conceited after his visionary experience of being caught up into the "third heaven" or "paradise" (2 Corinthians 12:1–10). If the "third heaven" is "paradise," then it is the place where Christ and the righteous dead dwell (Luke 23:43).

From the time of the church fathers to the present, commentators have proposed different solutions for the meaning of Paul's thorn in the flesh. The proposals are endless: headache, lust of the flesh, adversaries, malaria, poor eyesight, sorrow over his former life, the inevitable trials of missionary endeavors, a demonic adversary, defective speech, disappointment over the unbelief of his people (Jews), etc. One commentator has noted the two primary views are either Paul's opponents or some kind of physical suffering.

Study Questions

Unless otherwise noted, the questions are from the text in 2 Corinthians 12:5–10.

1. Why does Paul say he was afflicted with a thorn in the flesh? Have any of your life experiences served to keep you humble?

2. Note that Paul says he was "given a thorn in [the] flesh" (v. 7). This is called a "divine passive" and means that it was given by God. How has God worked through difficult experiences in your life to encourage dependence on him?

3. How would you harmonize the fact that the thorn in the flesh was from God, but Paul calls it "a messenger of Satan"?

4. In chapter 11:13–15, Paul refers to his opponents as Satan's servants, but he also gives a long list of his trials in 11:21–33. Do you think the context best supports the view that the thorn in the flesh was Paul's opponents or physical suffering? Why?

5. Do you think it was intentional that Paul did not specifically identify his thorn in the flesh? Why or why not?

6. What is the life lesson that Paul learned from his thorn in the flesh?

7. All of us experience troubling and persistent issues caused by our choices, other people, or circumstances. What is your thorn in the flesh?

8. What did Paul mean when he said, "when I am weak, then I am strong"?

9. Do you consider your thorn in the flesh a strength or weakness? Why should you consider it a strength?

10. Why do you think Paul stopped asking for deliverance after he had prayed three times? What does this teach us about prayer, and how would you harmonize this with Jesus' teaching on persistent prayer (Luke 11:5–10)?

Memory Verse: 2 Corinthians 12:8–10

Paul's Prayers

EPHESIANS

If you are like me, you struggle with the discipline of prayer. "I don't have time." "I'm too busy." "I don't know what to pray." "Why should I pray, when I can do something?" "Prayer doesn't seem to make a difference." These are some—certainly not all—of the excuses that I make for not praying.

One of my former colleagues was a man of prayer. He used 3 x 5 note cards to pray. He carried them with him, and I would see him periodically looking at one of the cards and bowing his head in silent prayer.

Paul was a man of prayer. He prayed for individuals (2 Timothy 1:2–3) and for entire churches (Colossians 1:9–14). I don't think he carried 3 x 5 note cards, but he recorded two of his prayers in Ephesians. Paul's prayers in 1:15–23 and 3:14–21 have helped remind me of the importance of prayer and how to pray for others.

Study Questions

Ephesians 1:15–23

1. 1:15. Why did Paul pray for the Ephesians? How did the Ephesians and how can we visibly show the strength of our faith?

2. 1:16–17.
   a. What two requests does Paul make for the Ephesians? How can you include these kinds of requests in your prayers?
   b. Why is it important that we grow in both our intellectual and experiential knowledge of God and pray that others may as well?

3. 1:18. How does it encourage you to know that God considers you his glorious inheritance?

4. 1:19–21. What was the ultimate revelation (display) of the greatness of God's power? Note: The "heavenlies" or "heavenly realms" is not a reference to heaven but to the spiritual realm where Christ now rules with absolute power and supreme authority.

5. 1:22–23. How does Paul say the church is now related to Christ, who is all powerful and fills the entire universe? How can we include this incomprehensible reality in our prayers for others?

Ephesians 3:14–21

6. 3:14. Do you think it is important that we kneel when praying? Why or why not? See 1 Timothy 2:8.

7. 3:16–17. What does it mean for Christ to make his home in our hearts?

8. 3:18–19. Why is it important that we understand the immensity of the love of Christ, especially in matters of relationships between people who are different?

9. 3:20–21. Paul concludes his prayer with a doxology of praise. What does Paul say in the doxology that should motivate us to pray rather than rely on our limited human effort?

General

10. What are some of the requests that we typically make that are not in Paul's prayers?

11. What two changes are you going to make in the way you pray after studying Paul's prayers?

Memory Verse: Ephesians 1:15–16

60

Slavery, Illegal Immigration, and Forgiveness

PHILEMON

Slavery was widespread in the Roman Empire. It's estimated that at one time there were a million slaves. Aristotle commented that slaves were "human tools."

Jesus did not address the issue of slavery directly, but in the synagogue at Nazareth he declared, "He has sent me to proclaim freedom for the prisoners and recovery of sight for the blind, to set the oppressed free, to proclaim the year of the Lord's favor" (Luke 4:18–19).

Paul gives instructions to masters and slaves in Ephesians 6:5–9 and Colossians 3:22–4:1. These passages are commonly applied to employer/employee relationships. Though there are some similarities, the relationships between employers and employees are not the same as masters and slaves.

Paul also wrote the epistle of Philemon as a real-life paradigm about how Christians should regard slaves. I would like for us to apply what Paul says in Philemon to the volatile and massive problem of illegal immigration.

Philemon was a dedicated and respected leader in the church at Colosse, located in Asia Minor (Philemon 1). One of his slaves, Onesimus, had run away and made his way to Rome. There he met Paul and trusted Christ as his Savior. He confessed that he was a runaway slave, but instead of challenging the institution of slavery Paul told Onesimus to return to Philemon. Runaway slaves could be severely punished or even executed. Paul, however, wrote the letter to encourage Philemon to treat Onesimus as a "dear brother" in the Lord (v. 16).

Study Questions

Questions on Illegal Immigration

1. Philemon 8–21. What are the similarities and differences between Onesimus's circumstances and those of people who have come into our country illegally?
2. Philemon 8–9, 14.
   a. What is the basis for Paul's appeal to Philemon?
   b. Why didn't Paul use his apostolic authority?
3. Philemon 10–16.
   a. Why didn't Paul establish a sanctuary church in Rome?
   b. What would Paul say to sanctuary churches today?
4. Philemon 17–18. What responsibility do we as Christians have to illegal immigrants?

Questions on Forgiveness

5. Philemon 8–9.
   a. Why is it difficult to forgive those who have offended us?
   b. What is the ultimate reason why we should forgive others?
6. Philemon 10.
   a. Though Philemon had the legal right to punish Onesimus, how did Paul encourage him to treat Onesimus?
   b. What can you do to forgive someone who has offended you?

7. Philemon 17–19; 1 Timothy 2:5–6. Many see in these verses a classic illustration of how Christ is the mediator between God and sinners.
   a. Why do we need a mediator?
   b. How is Christ our mediator?

Memory Verse: Philemon 16

61

Tithes and Offerings

I read a bumper sticker that said, "If you love Jesus, don't honk, tithe!" Though humorous, is it biblical? Only if you believe Christians are bound by the law of Moses!

What is tithing? Even before the time of Moses, we have references to the tithe (a tenth). Abraham paid a tithe to Melchizedek, the mysterious king and priest of Salem (Genesis 14:18–20). The law of Moses required the payment of tithes and offerings (Deuteronomy 12:6–7; 14:22–24). The obligation to give God a tenth continued through Old Testament history and the 400 years between the two testaments. In the last book of the Old Testament, the prophet Malachi indicts the people for cheating God and promises that he will bless them if they bring him their tithes and offerings (Malachi 3:6–12).

Most of the churches I have attended since I became a Christian have taught tithing. Some have even appealed to the passage from Malachi and assured people that God will bless them if they tithe, and if they don't they will suffer the consequences. Here's the catch! Tithing is a requirement under the law of Moses, and Jesus fulfilled the Law. The New Testament, especially Paul, makes it clear that Christians are not under the Law. We are under the New Covenant (Jeremiah 31:31–34; Mark 14:23–25). Plus, there are no commands in the New Testament to tithe. Almost all of the references are from the Gospels and negative. Jesus, for example, condemns the Pharisees for their hypocritical tithing (Matthew 23:23).

What then are the guidelines for Christian giving? Paul describes what I call "grace giving" in his admonition to the church at Corinth to complete the commitment they made to send an offering to the church in Jerusalem (2 Corinthians 8–9).

Study Questions

The following questions are all from 2 Corinthians 8–9 unless otherwise noted and will guide you in designing a paradigm (plan) for "grace giving."

1. 8:1. What does Paul call Christian giving? The term translated "grace" (*charis*) is the same word used for spiritual gifts (*charismata*). What does this suggest about "grace giving"?
2. 8:1–9. What two examples does Paul give of giving? How would you describe their giving?
3. 8:10–11. What amount does Paul tell the Corinthians to give? What does this mean for our giving in relation to tithing?
4. 8:12–16. What does Paul say about giving for the needs of others?
5. 8:16–24. Why does Paul say he entrusted Titus and his companion to take the offering to Jerusalem? What is Paul's concern about those handling the offering (vv. 20–21). What is the implication for those who are entrusted with money?
6. 9:1–5. Why did Paul boast about the Corinthians? What was his concern about the Corinthians' gift?
7. 9:6–10. What are two principles from the analogy of a farmer?
8. 9:10–14. What will believers in Jerusalem do when they receive the Corinthians' gift? Do you think people today consider these two responses when they give for the needs of others?
9. 9:15. What is the indescribable gift God has given to all believers? See John 3:16.

10. 1 Corinthians 16:1–4. When should believers give and what amount? Why do you think Paul encouraged regular, systematic giving?

11. Using information from above, can you put together a paradigm (plan) for "grace giving"?

Memory Verse: 2 Corinthians 9:13–15

62

Trustworthy Sayings

Though written by Paul, the epistles of 1 Timothy, 2 Timothy, and Titus, commonly called the Pastoral Epistles, contain an expression not found in his other epistles. Five times Paul inserts a "trustworthy saying" in the three epistles (1 Timothy 1:15; 3:1; 4:9; 2 Timothy 2:11; Titus 3:8).

For example, he writes in 1 Timothy 1:15, "Here is a trustworthy saying that deserves full acceptance: Christ Jesus came into the world to save sinners—of whom I am the worst."

What is the purpose of these sayings? One view is that the statements introduce authoritative teachings from the doctrinal traditions of the early church. The other view is that Paul used the expression to support the trustworthiness of his teaching. Whichever view is accepted, the purpose was the same—to emphasize correct doctrine and to counter the false teachers in the churches at Ephesus and Crete, where Timothy and Titus served respectively.

Study Questions

1. 1 Timothy 1:15–17.
   a. Why does Paul say Christ came into the world?
   b. Why do you think Paul refers to himself as the worst of sinners?
   c. How does Paul describe God (possibly Christ in verse 17)?
   d. Why are these characteristics of God important in relation to our salvation?

2. 2 Timothy 2:11–13.

   These verses could come from a hymn or confessional statement (possibly baptism) of the early church. Paul has incorporated the saying in his letter to encourage believers and warn unbelievers.

   a. What is the encouragement for believers in verse 11?
   b. What is the warning for people who only profess to know Christ in verse 12?
   c. What is the promise for believers in verse 13?
   d. Why will Christ remain faithful to believers even if they are unfaithful (disobedient and unproductive)?

3. Titus 3:8.

   a. What does Paul want Titus to emphasize in his teaching? Why is this important for Christians?
   b. What are some of the ways we can devote ourselves to doing good?

Memory Verse: Titus 3:8

PART 4

General Epistles

63

Faith without Works Is Dead

JAMES VERSUS PAUL

Though James is the most practical epistle in the New Testament, it is also problematic. Martin Luther called it a "right strawy epistle," and supposedly tore it out of his Bible and kept it in the fly leaf. He believed it was practical but not canonical. Why? James seems to contradict Paul. James says that "faith without works is dead" (2:26 KJV; see also 2:14–16), but Paul claims that a person "is justified by faith apart from the works of the law" (Romans 3:28).

Was Luther right? Are James and Paul contradictory? Should we tear James out of our Bibles? (The story that Luther did is probably apocryphal.) Or, is there a way to harmonize James and Paul? A little background will help. James wrote early in the history of the church to Jews who thought that because they had come to Christ by faith, they did not need to do anything to prove the genuineness of their faith. James reprimanded such people by saying, "Show me your faith without deeds, and I will show you my faith by my deeds" (James 2:18). In other words, James is teaching that works are evidence of true faith before others. Paul addressed a different issue. A large segment of his audience included Jews who struggled with salvation by grace through faith. They wanted to add the keeping of the Law to faith. Paul rejected that erroneous thinking and insisted that justification is by faith alone. God justifies "those who have faith in Jesus" (Romans 3:26). His perspective was justification before God.

James and Paul are complementary, not contradictory. We can be thankful for both perspectives. From Paul we know that we cannot save ourselves. We are justified by faith and not good works.

And James clarifies the nature of true faith. Saving faith expresses itself in works.

Study Questions

1. Ephesians 2:8–10. The heart of Paul's teaching is that salvation is a gift that can never be earned, but what does he say is the result of true faith (v. 10)? How are these verses in agreement with what James says about faith and works?
2. James 2:1–12. What are some of the ways we can show that our faith is genuine?
3. James 2:14–18. What are some of the differences between true faith and dead faith?
4. James 2:19–20. What is the difference between knowing about God and knowing God?
5. James 2:21–26. What two Old Testament persons did James use as illustrations of genuine faith? What did they do that made them remarkable examples of faith in action? How does their example motivate you to good deeds?
6. Romans 3:27; James 2:17. What is the relationship between faith and works in a balanced Christian life? How do you balance Paul's emphasis on faith and James's emphasis on works in your life?
7. Matthew 25:31–46. To what extent is helping the needy evidence of genuine faith? How do you and/or your church help the needy in your community?

Memory Verse: James 2:26; Galatians 5:6

64

Holy Spirit in the Epistles

The Gospels reveal the ministry of the Holy Spirit to a few individuals but primarily to Jesus. They also note Jesus' promise to send the Holy Spirit. Acts records the fulfillment of Jesus' promise and the work of the Holy Spirit in empowering, guiding, and confirming believers in their universal witness.

But it is in the Epistles that we find the most comprehensive account of the ministry of the Spirit. The following references give the multiple ministries of the Spirit to believers.

Study Questions

1. 1 Thessalonians 1:5–6. What does the Holy Spirit do when we witness to unbelievers?
2. Titus 3:5. What is the function of the Spirit in transforming believers into new people?
3. 1 Corinthians 6:18–20. What has happened to our bodies because we have trusted Christ as Savior? What would you say to a person who says, "I can do anything I want with my body because only my spirit matters"?
4. 1 Corinthians 2:10–16. What does the Spirit enable us to know that unbelievers can't know?
5. Galatians 3:1–5; Acts 19:1–6. How and when do believers receive the Holy Spirit?
6. Galatians 5:16–26. What does it mean to "walk in the Spirit"? How can you live a fruitful life?
7. Ephesians 1:12–14. What does the gift of the Spirit guarantee God will do for us? What would you say to a person who fears they may lose their salvation?

8. 1 Corinthians 12:4–11. What is the purpose of spiritual gifts? How can you know your spiritual gift and why is it important? Do you think most people know their spiritual gift?

9. Romans 8:26–27. How does the Spirit help us pray?

10. Romans 8:5–13. What will we do and not do if we are controlled by the Spirit of God?

11. Romans 8:9–11. What is the implication for the Trinity in Paul's interchange of titles, "Spirit of Christ" and "Spirit of God"?

12. 2 Peter 1:20–21. What did Peter believe about the Old Testament? How does this give you confidence that both the Old Testament and the New are the inspired Word of God?

13. 1 John 4:1–6. How do we determine if a person has the Spirit of God or the "spirit of antichrist" (a false spirit)?

14. 1 John 5:6–8. In this difficult passage, John is refuting a heretical teaching that Jesus was only a spirit-filled man. John gives a threefold witness to the person of Christ by combining the witness of the Spirit, Jesus' baptism, and his crucifixion. How does this passage support the belief that Jesus was truly the Son of God (both God and man)?

15. Revelation 1:4; 3:1; 4:5; 5:6. Most believe the "seven spirits" is a reference to the sevenfold Spirit of God. In Scripture the number seven is used as a symbol for perfection, and the reference to the sevenfold Spirit emphasizes the complete perfection of the Spirit. What are the different functions of the Spirit in these passages? See also Revelation 2:7. How does John view what he is writing to the churches?

Memory Verse: 1 Corinthians 12:7–11

65

Last Words of Peter

Peter's last spoken words are not recorded in Scripture. Peter was executed in the mid-sixties when Nero was emperor. Unlike Paul, who was a Roman citizen and could not be executed by crucifixion, Peter was crucified. According to church tradition he didn't think himself worthy to die in the same manner as the Lord, so the Romans granted Peter's request to be crucified upside down. Before his death Peter wrote 1 and 2 Peter from Rome.

Peter wrote his first epistle to instruct and encourage believers who were persecuted because of their radically different lifestyle. In his second epistle, he warns about false teachers and sternly denounces their erroneous teaching, especially the denial of the Lord's second coming.

For his last words, we will look at Peter's concluding remarks in his last epistle, 2 Peter.

Study Questions

2 Peter 3:1–18

In chapter 3, Peter refutes the teaching of scoffers who claimed that the delay in the second coming was evidence that God doesn't keep his promises. He assures believers that Christ will return and that they should eagerly anticipate his coming.

1. 3:3–4. Why do you think unbelievers mock Christians for believing in the Lord's return? How should we respond to people who ridicule us for believing in the second coming of Christ?

2. 3:5–7. What historical event does Peter give as evidence that God has judged the world in the past and will judge it in the

future? Why is it important that we remember that God is not only Creator but also Judge (2 Peter 2:9)?

3. 3:8–9. Why has the Lord withheld judgment on the world? What does this reveal about the character of God?

4. 3:10–13.
   a. What will happen to the present heavens and earth when the Lord returns?
   b. How does Peter exhort us to prepare for the second coming?
   c. How does holy and godly living hasten the Lord's coming?
   d. What does it mean to live "holy and godly lives"?
   e. What do you think the new heaven and new earth will look like, "where righteousness dwells"?

5. 3:14. The words *spotless* and *blameless* were used to describe animals that didn't have any defects and were acceptable as sacrifices to the Lord. Since we have been infused with "the divine nature" (2 Peter 1:4) God expects us to make every effort to be like Christ. How would you encourage a teenager to keep themselves morally pure?

6. 3:18. Peter's final words (benediction) are both an admonition and praise.
   a. How do we grow in grace and knowledge?
   b. *Glory* means "honor." How can you honor the Lord at home or in your work this week?

Memory Verse: 2 Peter 3:13–14

66

Melchizedek

Years ago I met with two young men who claimed their religious movement had priests who were descendants of Aaron. They were surprised when I said that I have a superior high priest. They asked, "Who?" I answered, "The Lord Jesus Christ, who is in the priesthood of Melchizedek," and showed them a couple of passages from the epistle of Hebrews. They didn't know how to answer.

To convince Jews who were struggling with their commitment to Christ, the writer of Hebrews argues for the superiority of Christ over the old covenant. One of his main arguments is the priesthood of Christ. He is a high priest in the order of Melchizedek (Hebrews 5:1–10), and gives reasons why the order of Melchizedek is superior to the Levitical priesthood (Hebrews 7:1–28).

Melchizedek first appears in Scripture in the story of Abraham. After the patriarch rescued his nephew who had been kidnapped by five kings, Abraham paid tithes to a mysterious king and priest named Melchizedek (Genesis 14:1–20). The only other reference is to the priesthood of Melchizedek in a messianic prophecy in Psalm 110, which Jesus quoted to support his claim that he was the Messiah and the Son of God (see Matthew 22:44–45; Mark 12:36–37; Luke 20:42–44). The prophecy is unique because it says that the Messiah will combine two offices both as a king (a royal descendant of David) and a priest (Psalm 110:1–4).

Study Questions

1. Hebrews 5:1–3. Why do we need a high priest?

2. Hebrews 5:4–6. Who appointed Christ as the High Priest? According to Psalm 2:7, why is Christ's appointment unique?

3. Hebrews 5:7–10.
   a. How did Christ qualify as a perfect High Priest? Speed read Leviticus 16 and note what the high priest had to do before he could make sacrifices for the sins of the people on the Day of Atonement.
   b. How does suffering teach obedience?
   c. Hebrews 12:7–13. What are the differences between a father's discipline and God's discipline?

4. Hebrews 7:8–19, 23–25.
   a. Why is the priesthood of Melchizedek superior to the Levitical priesthood?
   b. How would you respond to someone who claims their religious group has priests?

5. Hebrews 7:26–28.
   a. What are the differences between Christ and all other priests, particularly those under the old covenant?
   b. Why don't we need to offer sacrifices over and over to atone for our sins?

6. Hebrews 7:25; 8:1–2.
   a. Why can we be confident that our salvation is forever?
   b. Where does Christ minister as our high priest?
   c. What does the writer emphasize again about Jesus that makes his priesthood unique (see Psalm 110:4)?

—Optional

7. Hebrews 7:1–10.
   a. The writer's reasoning is based on the importance of family lineage in priesthood, making it somewhat difficult for us to understand, but what is his argument for the superiority of Melchizedek over Levi, a descendant of Abraham?

b. The reference to Melchizedek as a type of Christ's priesthood has been interpreted in two ways. One view is that Melchizedek was the preincarnate Christ because verse 3 implies that he was eternal. Others believe that Melchizedek was an actual king because all other types in the Old Testament are real historical people. Because we have no record of his birth or death it only seems like he was eternal. Which view do you take and why? Does it matter in the writer's argument?

Memory Verse: Hebrews 7:27

67

New Covenant

The prophet Jeremiah had the grievous task of warning Judah of the Babylonian exile, but the prophet also offered hope. He assured Judah that the exile was not the end of the nation, and promised that the Lord would make a new covenant with his people (Jeremiah 31:31–34). In contrast to the law of Moses, which regulated people's lives by external laws, the new covenant would bring about a spiritual transformation: "I will put my law in their minds and write it on their hearts. I will be their God, and they will be my people" (Jeremiah 31:33).

At the last Passover meal, Jesus anticipated the inauguration of the new covenant by the shedding of his blood on the cross: "Then he took a cup, and when he had given thanks, he gave it to them, saying, 'Drink from it, all of you. This is my blood of the covenant, which is poured out for many for the forgiveness of sins'" (Matthew 26:27–28). Jesus' death fulfilled the prophecy of Jeremiah and became the basis for salvation in the age of grace.

Two New Testament passages help us understand why the new covenant is crucial to God's unfolding plan of redemption. In 2 Corinthians 3, Paul defends his ministry by claiming that his ministry under the new covenant is superior to ministry under the old covenant (the law of Moses). His main point is that the reflection of God's glory on the face of Moses was only temporary, but believers are being permanently transformed into the glorious image of the Lord by the power of the Holy Spirit (2 Corinthians 3:18). The main argument in Hebrews 8–10 for the superiority of faith in Christ over keeping the Law is the nature of the new covenant. The writer argues that if the first covenant (the law of Moses) had been perfect, there would be no need for a new covenant (8:7–12). In contrast to sacrifices under the old covenant, which had to be repeated again and again, Christ made a sacrifice once for all (10:8–10).

Study Questions

1. Matthew 26:27–28. How does knowing that you are in a new covenant relationship with God affect how you live?
2. Romans 5:1–2. How do we enter into a new covenant relationship with God, and what are the blessings of our new covenant relationship?
3. Hebrews 7:20–28. Why is Jesus a better high priest than the priests under the old covenant? How is it helpful to think of Jesus as our high priest in our new covenant relationship with God?
4. Hebrews 9:13–15. Why can we have absolute confidence that our sins have been forgiven under the new covenant?
5. Hebrews 10:1–7. What was the purpose of sacrifices under the old covenant? According to this passage what was the purpose of Christ's humanity (human body)? What helps you to remember Christ's sacrifice for sins?
6. 2 Corinthians 3:12–18. In contrast to Moses under the old covenant, what is happening to us under the new covenant? What lifestyle practices help you to become more like Christ? What practices do you avoid?

Memory Verse: 2 Corinthians 3:18; Hebrews 10:10

68

Rest

The concept of spiritual rest is found in two passages in the New Testament. (Note: In the Old Testament rest is primarily physical, but in the New Testament it is spiritual.) In Matthew 11:28–30 Jesus promises rest to those who will put on his yoke, which is easy and light. In the epistle to the Hebrews, the author promises rest to those who persevere and do not harden their hearts as the Israelites did in the wilderness (3:7–19; 4:1–11).

In Matthew, Jesus draws on two Old Testament passages for his offer of rest. His promise follows an implicit claim of deity: "No one knows the Son except the Father, and no one knows the Father except the Son" (11:27) and precedes a Sabbath controversy that concludes with Jesus' claim that he is "Lord of the Sabbath" (12:1–8). In the Genesis account of creation, God rested on the seventh day and ordained it as a day of rest (Genesis 2:2–3). The Israelites were commanded to rest on the seventh day because "the Lord blessed the Sabbath day and made it holy" (Exodus 20:8–11). Jesus puts himself in the place of God when he promises to give rest to people burdened by the heavy yoke of religious legalism and when he claims he is "Lord of the Sabbath."

The background for the promise and warning in Hebrews is twofold. On the journey to the Promised Land, the Israelites rebelled at Kadesh and were unable to enter into the place of rest because of unbelief (Hebrews 3:7–19; Numbers 14). Second, the writer states that Israel entering the Promised Land under the leadership of Joshua did not fulfill God's promise of ultimate rest (Hebrews 4:8). Thus the writer assures his readers there remains a rest for the people of God (Hebrews 4:9), and he exhorts his readers not to harden their hearts but to make every effort to enter into that rest (Hebrews 4:10–11).

Study Questions

1. Matthew 11:28–30.
   a. Why did Jesus invite people to come to him for rest? What heavy burdens (religious requirements) do we put on people today?
   b. How does Jesus describe himself? Can you give an example of Jesus' humility from his early life? Why do you think it is important for Christians to be humble?
   c. What is Jesus' yoke? Why does he say it is easy and his burden light?
   d. Do you think it is easy to live the Christian life? Why or why not?

2. Hebrews 3:7–11.
   a. What were the consequences of rebellion for the children of Israel?
   b. Does God get angry with believers today? How would you describe his anger?
   c. What does the writer say we must do and not do in order to enter into rest?

3. Hebrews 4:1–11.
   a. 4:3. Who can enter into God's rest?
   b. 4:3–5. What Old Testament event is the background for rest?
   c. 4:11. What is the compelling reason for people to enter into God's rest?

—Optional

4. Who does the writer say is the author of Psalm 95 in 3:7? In 4:7? What does this suggest about the inspiration of Scripture?

Memory Verse: Matthew 11:28–30

69

Spirits in Prison

1 PETER

Do people get a second chance to believe in Christ after they die? Some believe that Christ offered a second chance to people in Hades after his resurrection: "After being made alive, he went and made proclamation to the imprisoned spirits" (1 Peter 3:19). There are three different interpretations of this difficult passage (1 Peter 3:18–22).

1) After his resurrection, Christ preached the gospel to people in Hades, giving them a second chance to believe. However, there is no scriptural evidence for a chance to trust Christ after death. Hebrews 9:27 states that judgment comes after death.
2) The preincarnate Christ preached through Noah to spirits now in prison awaiting final judgment. This view fits with the context but not the chronology of events. Peter says Christ preached after he was "made alive in the Spirit" (resurrected, 1 Peter 3:18).
3) Between his resurrection and ascension Christ announced (preached) victory to evil angels who sinned during the time of Noah (see Genesis 6:1–4; Jude 1:6). Christ did not offer them a second chance but announced victory over rebel angels imprisoned in gloomy dungeons in "hell" (2 Peter 2:4). The term in Greek is *tartarus* and was a popular term for the underworld. Scholars have explained it as "a subterranean place lower than Hades where divine punishment was meted out."* This view is supported by the context,

* F.W. Danker, W. Bauer, W.F. Arndt, and F.W. Gingrich, *A Greek-English Lexicon of the New Testament and Other Early Christian Literature*, 3rd Edition (Chicago: University of Chicago Press, 2000), 991.

chronology, and Jewish tradition. It would have been an encouragement to persecuted Christians to know that Christ was victorious over evil spirits.

Study Questions

1. 1 Peter 3:22.
   a. Why did Peter inform his readers about Christ's exaltation and victory over angels?
   b. How would Peter's teaching be comforting to Christians who suffer today?
2. 1 Peter 3:20. Why were people unwilling to repent in the time of Noah, and why are people unwilling to repent and trust Christ as Savior today?
3. 1 Peter 3:21. What does the flood symbolize? Why is baptism an appropriate symbol for cleansing from sin? What actually saves a person?
4. 1 Peter 3:21; Romans 6:1–4. How is baptism "the pledge of a clear conscience toward God"?
5. 2 Peter 2:4; Ephesians 6:10–12; Hebrews 1:14. Do you think we need more teaching about angels (good and evil)? Why or why not?
6. 1 Peter 3:22; Ephesians 1:21–23. Why do some Christians fear evil spirits (demons)? Why is it important to know that Christ rules victorious over all spiritual powers?

Memory Verse: 1 Peter 3:15–16

70

Unjust Suffering

SUFFERING AS A CHRISTIAN—1 PETER

The Gospels and Acts record the healing of people suffering from a variety of diseases. But in the Epistles most of the passages are about suffering related to persecution—unjust suffering. Because they refused to participate in the imperial cult and indulge in the immoral lifestyle of their pagan neighbors, Christians were despised and hated. In addition to physical persecution, they suffered economically and socially. They were also the targets of slander. In a group-oriented culture, honor and shame were important to one's social standing, and a loss of honor was devastating.

No one wants to suffer, but like Christians in the first century we will be persecuted for our faith. The New Testament assures us that when we suffer we are following in the footsteps of our Savior and that our response to persecution can actually help advance the kingdom of God.

In 1 Peter, the apostle explains how we should respond to unjust suffering and encourages us to remember that we are destined for eternal glory.

Study Questions

1. 1 Peter 1:6–7. What is one of the benefits of suffering? What is the analogy that Peter uses?

2. 1 Peter 2:13–16. Though Peter urges believers to submit to civil authorities, what are the limitations on obedience to government?

3. 1 Peter 3:13–17.
    a. Why do non-Christians slander Christians for their good behavior?
    b. Have you ever been criticized for doing good? How did you respond?
    c. What does it mean to honor Christ as Lord?
    d. How can we be prepared to tell others about our hope in Christ?
4. 1 Peter 3:16. Who is the ultimate example of unjust suffering? What is the difference between the suffering of Christ and our suffering?
5. 1 Peter 4:12–16. Why does Peter say we should not be surprised or ashamed when we suffer as Christians? Have you ever been in a situation where you felt ashamed because you were identified as a Christian? How did you respond?
6. How would you use 1 Peter 3:13–17 to help a high school student who was being ridiculed by her or his peers?
7. 1 Peter 5:8–9. Though Peter does not state it directly, who does he identify as the source of persecution? What are some of the ways that we can resist the devil?
8. 1 Peter 5:10–11. What is the new perspective that Peter gives on suffering? How is this a message of encouragement?

Memory Verse: 1 Peter 3:15–16

PART 5

Revelation

Babylon, Babylon

The ancient city of Babylon is referred to numerous times in the Old Testament, but Babylon is primarily a symbolic name for a godless empire that is the ultimate enemy of the people of God. In the New Testament, the term *Babylon* occurs in 1 Peter and the book of Revelation.

In his first epistle Peter sends greetings from the church in Babylon to the churches in Asia Minor: "She who is in Babylon, chosen together with you, sends you her greetings" (1 Peter 5:13). Some think Peter was writing from either a town in Egypt or the ancient city of Babylon on the Euphrates River. A few have suggested the greeting is from Peter's wife (not likely). If Peter was writing from Rome when Nero was persecuting Christians (ca 65 AD), there would have been a need for secrecy. The recipients would have known that *Babylon* was a code name for Rome, "the capital of the evil empire."

In Revelation, *Babylon* is a code name for a godless and seductive empire that attempts to dominate the world (14:8; 16:19; 17:5; 18:2, 10, 21). In chapters 17 and 18, John describes the destruction of this satanically inspired empire. There are three major views on this empire. One view is that all of the references are to Rome and describe the great struggle of believers against the Roman Empire in the first century (preterist view). Others believe the references are to evil empires throughout history (continuous view). A third view is that *Babylon* refers to the final political/religious system that will dominate the world prior to divine judgment (futuristic view). A combination of all three is a possibility.

Note: In stark contrast to *Babylon*, John describes the eternal dwelling place of believers as "the new Jerusalem" (Revelation 21).

Study Questions

1. Revelation 17:1–18. To justify God's judgment, John describes the sins of Babylon.
    a. How does John identify Babylon? Why does John use this imagery? How are nations in the world today like Babylon?
    b. In this passage John draws on imagery from the Old Testament in which the prophets repeatedly accused Israel of spiritual adultery for worshiping other gods. The classic example is God's command for Hosea to marry Gomer, an adulterous woman (Hosea 1:2), to symbolize Israel's spiritual adultery. Feminists have objected to the use of female imagery in this passage. Do you find it offensive? Why or why not?
    c. Revelation 17:3–6. In addition to prostituting herself to other gods, what was the other terrible sin of Babylon?
    d. What does God do to bring about the destruction of "the evil empire"? See 17:15–18.
    e. What assurance does this passage give us about God's plans and purposes?

2. Revelation 18:1–24. Using graphic poetic imagery, John describes the total destruction of Babylon.
    a. What sins are described in the chapter?
    b. What are God's people urged to do? See 18:4, 20.
    c. What are the lessons about the nature of sin and its consequences?
    d. What does the chapter reveal about the nature (character) of God?

Memory Passage: Revelation 19:1–2

72

Lamb of God

In a book that is about cosmic conflict and the ultimate victory of the Lord Jesus Christ, it seems strange that John refers to Christ as the Lamb of God, a title he uses twenty-seven times in the book of Revelation. He only uses the title two other times. While baptizing people John the Baptist saw Jesus approaching and cried out, "Look, the Lamb of God, who takes away the sin of the world!" (John 1:29). The next day John again called Jesus the "Lamb of God" (John 1:36).

There are two other references to Christ as a lamb, but not as a title. The Ethiopian eunuch was reading a messianic passage about the sacrificial lamb when he met Philip (Acts 8:32–33), and Peter said that people were redeemed (saved) by the precious blood of Christ, "a lamb without blemish or defect" (1 Peter 1:18–19).

The term *lamb* is used once of Jesus' disciples. Jesus sends them out with the warning: "Go! I am sending you out like lambs among wolves" (Luke 10:3, a different Greek word for *lamb*).

The term comes from the Old Testament. Lambs were the required sacrifice for the Passover (Exodus 12:1–13) and the daily sacrifices in the temple (Exodus 29:38–46). Both sacrifices symbolized atonement (a covering for sins) and anticipated the substitutionary death of Christ (Isaiah 53:7; Acts 8:32–35).

Study Questions

1. Revelation 5:1–7.
    a. What are the two titles for Christ, and what is paradoxical about them?

b. One of the unique features of the Christian experience is the paradox that weakness is strength, death is life, and defeat is victory. How have you experienced this paradox in your faith walk?

2. Revelation 5:6–14. The horns symbolize absolute power and authority (Daniel 7:24), and the eyes represent the Spirit, who has complete knowledge of what is taking place on the earth (Zechariah 4:10).
   a. Why is the Lamb worthy to open the scroll? The scroll contains the judgments which are about to be unleashed on the earth (seals, trumpets, and bowls).
   b. Why should we include a time of praise and worship in our devotions and in our church services?

3. Revelation 7:13–15.
   a. How are these verses a reminder of the divine paradox?
   b. Remembering the song "I Can Only Imagine," can you imagine what it will be like when you stand in the presence of God?

4. Revelation 14:3–5; 21:8, 27; 22:15. I'm not musical. I could never get into any choir, but apparently I will be in the heavenly choir. That's a scary thought!
   a. What are the symbols and images in these verses for believers (the redeemed)?
   b. Why do you think John emphasizes that those who lie will never get into heaven?
   c. How much do you value integrity and why?
   d. What are some of the ways we can "follow the Lamb" (live faithfully)?

5. Revelation 19:6–9. This wedding celebration will take place at the second coming of Christ. The "fine linen" represents the work of Christ. They are not our works but are given to us. Who has given them to us and why?

6. Revelation 21:22–23.
   a. Why isn't there a temple structure in heaven?
   b. What will it mean to have unlimited access to God?
7. Revelation 21:14, 27; Matthew 5:8. Why is your name written in the Lamb's book of life?

Memory Verse: Revelation 5:12

73

Last Words of John

John, the son of Zebedee, is known as the beloved disciple (see John 13:23). He and his brother James were fishermen but left the family business to follow Jesus (Matthew 4:21–22). He was one of Jesus' closest companions, witnessed the transfiguration (Matthew 17:1–5), and was with Jesus when he prayed in the garden of Gethsemane (Matthew 26:36–46). John and Peter followed Jesus when he was arrested, but John was the only apostle to actually witness the crucifixion (John 19:25–27). He and Peter were the first of the apostles to discover the empty tomb (John 20:1–10). After the resurrection, he was arrested along with Peter but released (Acts 4:1–22). John eventually became a leading member of the church in Jerusalem. Later in life, he was exiled to the island of Patmos (Revelation 1:8), and according to tradition was the only apostle to die of natural causes.

John wrote the fourth Gospel, three epistles, and the book of Revelation, which is technically an epistle. The book of Revelation, written while John was in exile on the island of Patmos, records his last words.

The book was written to inform and encourage Christians who were experiencing violent persecution near the end of the first century. The emperor Domitian was a devil. He insisted that everyone worship him as a "god." Jews and Christians who refused were arrested, brutally tortured, and sadistically executed.

John assures believers that God is in absolute control of history, that Jesus is victorious over all evil powers in heaven and earth, and that they will ultimately reign forever with God and the Lord Jesus.

Study Questions

Revelation 1:1–11—The Prologue or Introduction

1. 1:1–11. What new information did you discover about God, Christ, and the Holy Spirit?

2. 1:5. What is John's threefold description of Christ? How can you honor Christ?

3. 1:7–8. To what extent do you anticipate (look for) the coming of Christ? What are some of the distractions that hinder us from longing for the coming of Christ and experiences that increase our anticipation of the Lord's return?

4. 1:10. The reference to "the Lord's Day" can mean either Sunday (the day of Jesus' resurrection) or the day John received the revelation. Why is it important for believers to gather on Sunday or another day of the week for worship?

Revelation 22:6–21—The Epilogue or Conclusion

5. 22:6–7. What are the promises in the seven "beatitudes" (blessings) in Revelation (22:7; 1:3; 14:13; 16:15; 19:9; 20:6; 22:14)?

6. 22:8–9; Matthew 4:10. Why shouldn't we worship angels? What are some of the reasons God alone deserves our/your worship?

7. 22:10–11. John's statement about allowing people who are vile to continue to do evil is puzzling. John's point is that if people do not respond to the warnings in the book and repent, then they will continue to sin. Plus, John is not teaching salvation is by works; rather he is emphasizing that righteous deeds show that our confession of faith is genuine. What would you say to a person who claims they are a believer but persists in a sinful lifestyle?

8. 22:17–19. In spite of John's warning and the orthodox church's recognition of the canon of Scripture, throughout history individuals and groups have attempted to delete sections of the Bible and add other books to it. Why do you think people want to add or subtract from the Bible?

9. 22:20–21. How can you be a faithful witness to the grace of the Lord Jesus Christ?

Memory Verse: Revelation 22:20

74

Letters to the Seven Churches

John was in exile when he wrote to churches in the Roman province of Asia Minor (modern-day Turkey). Christianity faced two existential threats near the end of the first century (AD 90). The letters to the seven churches were written to encourage steadfastness because of the threats of persecution and false teaching.

We don't know the exact origin of these churches, but they were probably started as a result of Paul's three-year ministry in Ephesus (Acts 19:1–20:1, esp. 19:10). In a clockwise direction the letters are addressed to the churches of Ephesus, Smyrna, Pergamum, Thyatira, Sardis, Philadelphia, and Laodicea (Revelation 2:1–3:22). The strengths and weaknesses of these churches are characteristics of congregations throughout history and would be typical of churches today.

In the letter to the church at Ephesus we see the standard pattern for each of the letters (2:1–7):

Command to write (2:1a)
Description of the Son of Man (from the vision of Christ in 1:17–20) (2:1b)
Commendation (2:2–3)
Complaint (2:4)
Correction (2:5–6)
Promise (2:7)

Not all of these features are present in all of the messages. For example, there is no complaint in the letter to the church at Smyrna (2:8–11).

Study Questions

1. Revelation 2:1–7—To Ephesus
   a. What is the complaint?
   b. How would you explain John's admonition to repent to a believer who has drifted (fallen) away from Christ?

2. Revelation 2:8–11—To Smyrna
   a. How is Jesus described? Why was this a comforting truth for the church?
   b. How is this comforting for Christians today?

3. Revelation 2:12–17—To Pergamum
   a. To what Old Testament person are the false teachers compared? For background information, see Numbers 22:2–6 and 25:1–3.
   b. What is manna (see Exodus 16:11–15)? What did Jesus say about himself in John 6:32–33?

4. Revelation 2:18–29—To Thyatira
   a. What was the complaint?
   b. Who was Jezebel? See 1 Kings 16:31–33.
   c. What can we do to protect ourselves from the kinds of sins listed in verses 20–21?

5. Revelation 3:1–6—To Sardis
   a. How is Christ described in this letter? The reference to "the seven spirits of God" has Trinitarian implications. The number seven refers to the perfection of the Holy Spirit, the one who has the Spirit is Christ (cf. Revelation 1:20), and the Spirit is the Spirit of God.
   b. What was the reputation of the church? What do you think this means for churches and individuals today?

6. Revelation 3:7–13. The church of Philadelphia was persecuted by both Romans and Jews (synagogue of Satan).
   a. What element from the standard format is missing?

b. What does Jesus promise Christians who persevere through adversity? What are some of the trials that Christians experience today?

7. Revelation 3:14–20. Laodicea was one of three cities in the Lychus Valley. In contrast to Hierapolis and Colossae, the water supply in Laodicea was brackish. Fresh water was brought into the city via an aqueduct, but by the time it arrived the water was lukewarm.
   a. What did Jesus mean by "lukewarm"? How can you know if your relationship with Christ is lukewarm?
   b. Laodicea was a major commercial and banking center, and the Laodiceans were known for the use of a medicinal ointment for the eyes. What did Jesus mean when he told the church to buy gold and white clothes and put salve (ointment) on their eyes?
   c. What two images are used for the restoration of fellowship with Jesus? How do you sustain your fellowship with Jesus?

Key Passage: Revelation 1:17–20

75

Seals, Trumpets, and Bowls

Because of the apocalyptic imagery in the book of Revelation, it is admittedly difficult to understand; but most will agree that however we interpret the details it is about the ultimate victory of the Lamb (the Lord Jesus Christ). Though Christians suffer and die, those who persevere will enjoy life forever in the presence of God and the Lamb. Evil tyrants who have viciously persecuted Christians will not go unpunished. They will suffer the wrath of God and be cast into a lake of fire. The Lamb, who was slain, will receive all glory and power.

After the introduction (1:1–21) and the letters to the seven churches (2:1–3:22), John is caught up into heaven, where he sees angels and elders worshiping God, who is seated on his throne and holding a sealed scroll in his right hand (4:1–5:1). At first John is distressed because no one is worthy to open the scroll, but then Christ (the Lamb) steps forward and takes the scroll. He is worthy to open it because of his sacrificial death (5:2–14). The scroll contains the judgments that are about to be unleashed on the earth in a series of seals, trumpets, and bowls (Revelation 6:1–16:21).

These judgments come at the end of the present age and precede the coming of Christ to establish his eternal kingdom (19:11–21). Some believe the judgments occur during a seven-year period of tribulation that brings the present age to a dramatic conclusion.

The sequence in which the judgments are recorded gives the impression they are chronological. The seventh seal judgment holds the seven trumpet judgments, and the seventh trumpet judgment contains the seven bowl judgments. I take a different view. Because each series of judgments concludes with the coming of Christ, I believe they are executed in three concurrent cycles with increasing intensity (6:15–17; 14:14–20; 16:16–21). Between the sixth and seventh judgments in each series, John inserts an interlude that gives additional information about the cosmic drama that is taking place on earth and heaven.

***Six Seal Judgments** (6:1–17)*
Interlude (7:1–17)
Six Trumpet Judgments (In the seventh seal judgment (8:1–9:21)
Interlude (10:1–14:20)
Seven Bowl Judgments (In the seventh trumpet judgment) (15:1–16:21)
No Interlude

Study Questions

1. Revelation 5:1–10. Why was the Lamb qualified to open the sealed scroll? How much emphasis does your church place on witnessing to other nations and people groups?

2. Revelation 6:1–8. The four horses and their riders represent the political and military powers of this world. Why would it be a tragic mistake for people to put their hopes in the kingdoms of this world?

3. Revelation 7:9–17. How would you encourage people who live in countries where Christians are persecuted and killed for their faith?

4. Revelation 8:1–9:21. Which of the trumpet judgments are similar to the plagues on the Egyptians? See Exodus 7:8–11:10.

5. Revelation 9:20–21. Why did people refuse to repent even after the trumpet judgments?

6. Revelation 11:1–14. Though many have attempted to identify the two witnesses, it is best not to speculate. What

happens to them? How does their experience mirror the experience of some of the prophets and the Lord Jesus Christ?

7. Revelation 12:1–13:18. This passage looks back to the first century and forward to a terrible time of persecution. How many individuals are identified in the passage? Some refer to these three individuals as "Satan's unholy trinity."

8. Revelation 13:8–10. What is the difference between unbelievers and believers?

9. Revelation 16:1–21. The bowl judgments are the most severe, yet how do people respond?

10. What do these judgments reveal about the character of God?

Memory Verse: Revelation 5:11–12

PART 6

Doctrine

Angels

Angels are spiritual beings and active participants in the cosmic plan of redemption.

Angels were active in the life of Christ. The angel Gabriel announced the births of John the Baptist and Jesus (Luke 1:11–20; 1:26–37). The angel of the Lord proclaimed the birth of the Messiah to shepherds and then was joined by a host of angels praising God (Luke 2:8–15). An angel warned Joseph of Herod's intention to kill his son (Matthew 2:13). Angels cared for Jesus after he was tempted (Matthew 4:11; Mark 1:12–13). The angel of the Lord opened the tomb of Jesus and informed the women that Jesus had risen from the dead (Matthew 28:1–7; Mark 16:1–8; Luke 24:1–7; John 20:11–13).

Angels are not eternal. They were created to serve God's people (Hebrews 1:14). Though heavenly beings, they are inferior to the Son and worship him (Hebrews 1:6). They are highly intelligent but not all-knowing (1 Peter 1:12).

Jesus taught that angels minister in heaven on behalf of believers and serve as witnesses with God and Christ to the affairs of the church (Matthew 18:10; 1 Timothy 5:21; and possibly 1 Corinthians 11:10). Angels assured the apostles of Jesus' return from heaven (Acts 1:9–11). The angel of the Lord released the apostles from public jail (Acts 5:17–25). When Peter was arrested, he was set free by the angel of the Lord (Acts 12:1–11). After his release Peter went to the house where the disciples had been praying, but they were so disbelieving they thought it must be his personal angel (Acts 12:12–17). When Herod Agrippa I accepted worship, the angel of the Lord afflicted him with a terminal disease (Acts 12:23).

The ministry of angels will continue into eternity. They will accompany Christ when he returns to gather believers and judge the wicked (Matthew 24:31; 2 Thessalonians 1:7). Angels will separate the wicked from the righteous at the end of the age (Matthew 13:40–43).

Angels and believers will unite to worship God and Christ in heaven (Hebrews 12:22–24).

Some angels have rebelled against God and have aligned themselves with Satan (Ephesians 6:11–12; 1 Timothy 4:1). Like Satan, they are destined for eternal punishment (Matthew 25:41; 2 Peter 2:4; Jude 1:6).

Study Questions

1. Hebrews 1:14. How do angels minister to believers today? How does knowing that angels were created to serve believers assure you of your importance to God?

2. Genesis 1:31; 2 Peter 2:4. How did God describe his work of creation? Though not stated in Scripture, when is it most likely that angels rebelled against God? What does this suggest about the unseen world (the spiritual realm)?

3. Revelation 12:7–8; 20:1–3. How do angels function in God's grand plan of redemption? Why should we be aware but not fear fallen angels (demons)?

4. Mark 1:12–13. Why do you think angels ministered to Jesus after he was tempted?

5. Acts 12:15. Do you think that each of us has a personal angel, perhaps guardian angel?

6. Acts 8:26; 10:3–6; 12:6–10; 27:23–24. Though spiritual beings, angels can apparently assume human form. Do you think angels appear to people today? How would you respond if an angel were to appear to you?

7. 1 Corinthians 6:3. How do you feel about judging angels? Look at the context of 1 Corinthians 6:1–6. What is Paul's point about our value and significance as human beings created in the image of God?
8. Colossians 2:18–19. Why shouldn't we worship or pray to angels?
9. 1 Timothy 5:21. What difference does it make in how you live knowing that in addition to God and Christ, angels are watching you?

Memory Verse: Hebrews 1:14

77

Antichrist

MAN OF LAWLESSNESS/THE BEAST OUT OF THE SEA

The term *Antichrist* is used by some Christians to identify an incredibly powerful and evil individual who will appear at the end of the age, forcing people to worship him and viciously persecuting anyone who refuses. However, the title *Antichrist* is not actually used in Scripture to identify this person. In his first epistle, John refers to "the antichrist" and "many antichrists" to expose those who deny that Jesus is the Son of God (1 John 2:18, 22; 4:3), but he is not referring to the Antichrist who will oppose God and persecute Christians prior to the coming of "the day of the Lord" (2 Thessalonians 2:2).

Paul uses the phrase "man of lawlessness" to describe the appearing of a person who will profane the temple by claiming that he is God (2 Thessalonians 2:3–4). Though he attempts to overthrow God, he will be destroyed by the splendor of Christ's coming (2 Thessalonians 2:8). In the book of Revelation, John identifies the same individual as "a beast coming out of the sea" (13:1–10). The dragon (Satan) empowers this beast and "a second beast, coming out of the earth" (13:11–18) to force people to worship him. Both beasts are captured and thrown into a lake of fire when Christ returns as King of kings and Lord of lords (Revelation 19:11–21).

Some believe the Antichrist is the one who commits "an abomination that causes desolation" (Daniel 9:27), and that Jesus refers to this same person when he predicts the desecration of the temple (Matthew 24:15).

Study Questions

1. 1 John 2:18, 22; 4:1–3. Why does John use the term *antichrists* to describe false teachers? Do you think there are people today who could be called "antichrists"?

2. 2 Thessalonians 2:1–8. Throughout history many have identified the Antichrist as a historical person. The attempts include one of the Roman Emperors in the first century, one of the popes, cruel dictators like Adolph Hitler, Joseph Stalin, Sadam Hussein, and others. What are some of the dangers of doing this? What is Paul's emphasis in 2 Thessalonians 2:13–14?

3. Revelation 13:1–18. In addition to the beast out of the sea (Antichrist), who are the other two creatures John describes in this chapter? What are their actual identities? God exists as a trinity of the Father, Son, and Holy Spirit. Some have noted that these three represent a satanic and unholy trinity. Why do you think Satan would attempt to duplicate the true trinity of Father, Son, and Holy Spirit?

4. 2 Thessalonians 2:9–12. How does the man of lawlessness do the work of Satan? How does Paul describe his miracles? How do you distinguish truth from lies?

5. 1 John 2:18–19. What did John say the antichrists had done that proves they were not true believers? How important do you think it is to remain connected to a local church? Is it possible for a person who has left the church (rejected Christianity) to return to Christ? Why or why not?

6. 1 John 4:1–3. How does John distinguish between a person who has the spirit of the antichrist and one who has the Spirit of God? Why is it important to believe that Jesus had a real human body (his humanity was as genuine as his deity)?

7. 2 Thessalonians 2. It is obvious that Paul believed that God is in absolute control of history and that he will ultimately rescue his people and destroy the powers of evil and lawlessness. How important is it to believe that God is sovereign and in total control of history and everyday life?

Memory Verse: 2 Thessalonians 2:8

Apostle

Apostle (*apostolos*) means "sent one" or "messenger." In a general sense, it is used only three times in the New Testament. For example, Paul calls Epaphroditus a "messenger" (*apostolos*) (Philippians 2:25; see also John 13:16 and 2 Corinthians 8:23). The more frequent use is for a special office with delegated authority. Jesus commissioned twelve of his disciples as "apostles" (Matthew 10:1–4; Mark 3:13–19; Luke 6:12–16), and Paul claims that he was also appointed by Christ as an apostle (Romans 1:1).

There were obviously apostles in the early church, and this raises two questions about apostles today. One: What were the qualifications for an apostle? And two: Are there apostles in the church today?

Study Questions

1. Luke 6:12–16.
   a. What did Jesus do before he chose twelve apostles? Why should we pray before making important decisions?
   b. From the large number of his disciples, why did Jesus choose twelve as apostles? See Matthew 19:28.
2. Mark 3:13–15. Mark emphasizes that Jesus came to overthrow the kingdom of Satan. What delegated authority did Jesus give to the Twelve and why? What does it mean for us today to be representatives of Jesus?
3. Acts 1:21–22.
   a. What were the qualifications for a replacement for Judas?

b. Acts 1:23–26. How did the followers of Jesus select a replacement? Why would we or why wouldn't we use this method for making decisions? Who ultimately made the decision about a twelfth apostle? How can we discern the Lord's will today?

c. Galatians 1:1. Paul claimed that he was an apostle. Why was he qualified to be appointed as an apostle? See Acts 9:1–19.

d. Is it possible for anyone today to qualify as an apostle? How would you respond to a religious group who claims they have apostles today?

4. Acts 14:14; Galatians 1:19.

   a. In addition to the Twelve and Paul, what other two men are identified as apostles? This raises the question: Could others have been appointed as apostles? Though Ephesians 4:11 lists apostles as ministers in the early church, what does Paul state in 1 Corinthians 15:7–8 about his apostleship?

   b. Since the New Testament seems to indicate that Paul was the last "official" apostle, what is our authoritative source for teaching today? See 2 Timothy 3:16–17.

5. 1 Timothy 5:17–18. Though we don't have official apostles today, how can we honor and support the leaders in our church?

Memory Verse: Acts 1:21–22

79

Ascension

On the night he was arrested, Jesus prayed for the restoration of the divine glory he shared with his Father before the incarnation: "And now, Father, glorify me in your presence with the glory I had with you before the world began" (John 17:5). Jesus' prayer was answered forty days after his resurrection: "'Men of Galilee,' they said, 'why do you stand here looking into the sky? This same Jesus, who has been taken from you into heaven, will come back in the same way you have seen him go into heaven'" (Acts 1:11).

Study Questions

The following passages reveal why the ascension is important:

1. John 17:1–5; Hebrews 10:12–14. How do we know that Jesus' death on the cross fulfilled his mission to save us from our sins?

2. Acts 1:9–11. How would you answer a person who claims the second coming of Christ was fulfilled on the Day of Pentecost when Jesus gave the Holy Spirit to his followers?

3. John 14:1–3. How does Jesus' promise support the belief that heaven is a place and not a state of being? Does it matter that we don't know the location of heaven? Why?

4. Philippians 2:5–11. How does this passage support the belief that Jesus has been glorified as both God and man and not merely as deity?

5. Romans 8:28–30. Why does the glorification of Jesus as the unique God-man give us hope for glorification? Would we have hope if only Jesus' deity had been restored to glory?
6. Hebrews 4:14–16. What is Jesus' current ministry? How does it help to know that you have a high priest ministering on your behalf before the throne of God?

Memory Verse: Philippians 2:11–13

80

Church

Though there are many different ways to define the church, I define it as "a supernatural community of believers empowered by the Holy Spirit, devoted to one another in love, and committed to a universal witness."

After Peter declared that Jesus was the Son of God, the Lord promised that he would build his church: "And I tell you that you are Peter, and on this rock I will build my church, and the gates of Hades will not overcome it" (Matthew 16:18). Protestant interpreters believe the "rock" refers to Jesus not Peter.

Though the word *church* (*ekklesia,* "called out") is not used in Acts 2, most recognize the Day of Pentecost as the birthday of the church. When thousands of Jews were in Jerusalem, Jesus gave the Holy Spirit to his followers as he had promised and three thousand believed Peter's message (Acts 2:1–41). As more and more people believed, they were added to those who had initially received the Spirit (Acts 2:47; 4:4; 6:1). Plus, as the church broke through ethnic barriers, Luke emphasizes that Samaritans and Gentiles received the same Holy Spirit as the Jews on the Day of Pentecost (Acts 8:17; 10:44–46).

The description Luke gives of the church at Troas suggests they met in a home, and the church at Rome met in the home of Priscilla and Aquila (Acts 20:7–12; Romans 16:3–5). The church at Antioch commissioned Paul and Barnabas for the first missionary journey (Acts 13:1–3). Paul addressed his epistles to local churches (1 Corinthians 1:2; 1 Thessalonians 1:1). John wrote to the seven churches in Asia Minor (Revelation 1:11).

Though the early church met mostly in homes, the church exists in multiple dimensions. Paul identifies the universal dimension of the church when he writes that Christ loved the church and died for it (Ephesians 5:25–27). As the body of Christ the church also has a cosmic dimension: "And the church is his body; it is made full and complete by Christ, who fills all things everywhere with himself" (Ephesians 1:23 NLT). The writer of Hebrews includes both the living and those who have died in a heavenly dimension of the church (Hebrews 12:22–24).

Study Questions

1. Matthew 16:17–19.
   a. Who did Jesus say would build the church?
   b. What is the problem when people and pastors identify the church as "my church"?
   c. Who is the church's greatest enemy? What did Jesus promise?
   d. "Keys" are a figure of speech for the gospel. No person has the authority to include or exclude anyone from heaven. If people are either granted or denied access to heaven based on their response to the gospel, why is it important that we get the gospel message right?
2. Matthew 28:18–20.
   a. What is the church's mission?
   b. How can your church improve its effectiveness in fulfilling the Great Commission? How can you help?
3. Acts 5:1–16. After Peter announced judgment on Ananias and Sapphira, Luke says, "Great fear gripped the entire church and everyone else who heard what had happened" (NLT). In his commentary on Acts, G. Campbell Morgan said, "The result was not only fear; it was power."* After this incident, many were healed. Why is it important for a

* G. Campbell Morgan, *The Acts of the Apostles* (Grand Rapids, MI: Revell, 1934), 155.

church to keep itself free from sin? How does your church deal with sin?

4. Hebrews 10:24–25. Why is it important for us to meet regularly with other believers?
5. Hebrews 13:1–3, 15–16. What are four functions of a church?

Memory Verse: 1 Timothy 3:14–15

81

Cosmic Christ

"Don't taste!" "Don't touch!" "Submit to circumcision." "Worship angels." "These are the things that will make you spiritual," said the false teachers in the church at Colosse. (See Colossians 2:16–20.) Such teaching was confusing to young Christians who had believed the good news about Christ.

We don't know the exact origin and nature of the Colossian heresy. We know it included elements of Jewish legalism, Eastern mysticism, Gentile asceticism, and possibly emperor worship; however, the most dangerous aspect of the heresy was the undermining of the supremacy of Christ. The heretics claimed that Christ was insufficient for salvation and spiritual growth; other spiritual beings were needed.

While under house arrest in Rome (Paul's first imprisonment), Paul wrote to correct misunderstandings about Christ and assure the Colossian believers of the preeminence of Christ over every authority and power in the universe. In Colossians 1:15–20 he makes seven remarkable statements about the person and work of Christ. This passage has been labeled "the Cosmic Christ" because Paul describes Christ as preeminent over the entire cosmos.

Study Questions

1. Colossians 1:15–20. What are the seven statements Paul makes about Christ? How has this passage helped or changed your understanding of the person and work of Christ?

2. Colossians 1:15. What does it mean that Christ is "the image of the invisible God"? See Hebrews 1:3 and John

14:9. Why is it important for Christ to be the perfect revealer of God?

3. Colossians 1:15. What is the meaning of "firstborn"? It does not mean Christ was the first created being as some erroneously claim. Paul would have used a different Greek word had he meant "first created being."

   Answer: "Firstborn" means that Christ has the highest priority and total superiority over all of creation. See Psalm 89:27.

   *In a debate about the person of Christ in the early church, one of the church fathers stated that Christ "is not a creature, but the Creator of the creatures."**

4. Colossians 1:16. How would you answer the person who says Christ was the first created being, and then he created all other things? Note: The word *other* is not in the passage.

5. John 1:3; Hebrews 1:2. What do these two passages reveal about Christ and creation?

6. Colossians 1:18. How does Paul describe Christ's relationship to the church? How does this influence your understanding and involvement in your local church?

7. Colossians 1:19. What does Paul say God was pleased to do? Why was this important for the church at Colosse, which was threatened by false teachers claiming that Christians needed other spiritual beings to know God? How has Christ revealed God to you?

8. Colossians 1:20–22. What has God reconciled (made peace) to himself through the death of Christ? What does it mean to you that you are now a friend with God?

* Lynn H. Cohick, "Colossians," in Gary M. Burge and Andrew E. Hill, eds., *The Baker Illustrated Bible Commentary* (Grand Rapids, MI: Baker Books, 2012), 1403.

9. Colossians 1:22–23.
   a. What was God's purpose in reconciling us to himself?
   b. Because of what God has done through his Son, what does Paul say we must do as believers? What does it mean to "continue in your faith"?

Memory Verse: Colossians 2:10

Devil (Satan)

We have an enemy. His two primary names are Satan (Hebrew ***satan***, "adversary" and the devil (Greek ***diabolos***, "slanderer"). The name *devil* is used only in the New Testament and occurs thirty-three times (Matthew 4:1; 25:41; John 13:2; Ephesians 6:11; James 4:7; Revelation 12:9, et.al.).

Satan is a powerful angel who was created but rebelled against God (John 8:44). We have only glimpses of his malicious intentions in the Old Testament, but he is fully exposed as the diabolical enemy of God in the New.

The devil tempted Jesus to defy the will of God and promised him the kingdoms of this world in exchange for worship (Matthew 4:1–11). Jesus warned that an enemy (the devil) will try to disrupt the growth of the kingdom (Matthew 13:19). Peter was influenced by Satan when he tried to discourage Christ from his sacrificial death on the cross (Matthew 16:22–23). Judas was under the total control of Satan when he agreed to betray Jesus (Luke 22:3–6). Satan filled the heart of Ananias and Sapphira to lie (Acts 5:1–3). Satan tempts believers to sin (1 Corinthians 7:5). He schemes to destroy relationships in the church (2 Corinthians 2:9–11). Peter describes the devil as a roaring lion prowling around looking for prey (1 Peter 5:8). John warns that the difference between the children of God and the children of the devil is love and hate (1 John 3:10).

The devil is powerful, deceptive, and dangerous, but believers have nothing to fear. Jesus resisted Satan with Scripture (Matthew 4:1–11). Paul urges believers to courageously stand against the devil (Ephesians 6:10–18). James promises that if we resist Satan he will flee from us (James 4:7). John assures us that the devil is destined for eternal punishment (Revelation 20:10).

Study Questions

His Origin and the Origin of Sin

1. Ezekiel 28:11–19; Isaiah 14:12–14. Though it has been much debated, many believe these two passages contain a double reference to the kings of Tyre and Babylon and Satan, the evil power behind the two godless kings. Why is the sin of pride so dangerous, and how can we avoid it?

2. Genesis 1:31; 2 Corinthians 11:3; 1 John 3:8. What is the origin of sin? Why is it impossible for a true believer to continue sinning?

His Strategy and Activity

3. Genesis 3:1–7. How did Satan create doubt in the mind of Eve? What teachings (commandments) of Scripture do you doubt? What is your strategy for overcoming doubt about the goodness of God?

4. 1 Corinthians 7:5. Satan apparently uses the weakness of the flesh (our sinful human nature) to entice people to sin. 1 Thessalonians 4:1–8. How can we honor God with our bodies?

5. 2 Corinthians 11:12–15. Satan and his followers oppose the kingdom of God by disguising themselves as servants of Christ. How can you identify those who claim they are Christians but are actually agents of Satan?

The Devil and Believers

6. When tempted, Jesus resisted the devil and on the cross defeated him (Matthew 4:1–11; Ephesians 2:1–9). How can we resist and defeat the devil?
   a. Romans 16:20; Genesis 3:15. What has God promised that assures us of victory over Satan?

b. Ephesians 4:20–27. What attitudes do you need to renew to keep the devil from exploiting them to cause you to sin?
c. James 4:7. What does it mean to "humble yourselves before God" (NLT)? How do we resist the devil?

The Devil's Doom

7. Matthew 25:41; Revelation 20:10. How does knowing that Satan is doomed encourage you in resisting temptation?

Memory Verse: James 4:7

83

Eternal Punishment or Annihilationism?

In some ways, it is more difficult to imagine conscious eternal punishment for the wicked than it is eternal blessing for the righteous; however, the New Testament consistently warns of eternal punishment for the wicked.

Jesus taught that the wicked will be separated from the righteous and the wicked will be thrown into a fiery furnace where they will suffer forever (Matthew 13:47–51). In the story of the rich man and Lazarus, the rich man is fully aware that he is in a place of torment and asks Abraham to send Lazarus to warn his five brothers (Luke 16:19–31). Paul assures the Thessalonians that those who do not know God and have persecuted them will be punished with "everlasting destruction" (2 Thessalonians 1:8–10). Peter says that God cannot be fooled: "The Lord knows how to rescue the godly from trials and to hold the unrighteous for punishment on the day of judgment" (2 Peter 2:9). John describes the fate of those who worship the beast (unbelievers): "And the smoke of their torment will rise forever and ever. There will be no rest day or night for those who worship the beast and its image, or for anyone who receives the mark of its name" (Revelation 14:11).

I recently attended a theological conference, and one of the presenters read a paper on annihilationism. Like the presenter, some evangelical Christians believe eternal punishment is inconsistent with the justice of a loving God. They believe that unbelievers will be destroyed either immediately after death or after a period of just suffering.

Study Questions

1. John 3:16–21. How do you reconcile the love and justice of God with the condemnation of the wicked?

2. Luke 13:22–30. Jesus uses the imagery of the messianic feast to describe the state of the wicked and righteous. How do you think people will feel when they are thrown out because they were not invited?

3. Luke 16:19–31. "Abraham's side" (NIV) is a figure of speech for God's kingdom.
   a. What is the point in the parable about a person's state after death?
   b. What would you say to a person who says, "I'm not sure about trusting Christ as Savior now. I'll decide later"?
   c. 16:31. Why do some people refuse to repent even when they have the evidence of Scripture and the miracle of Jesus' resurrection?

4. 2 Thessalonians 1:8–10.
   a. What is the reason for the judgment of some and the salvation of others?
   b. What message would you explain to an unbeliever? See 1 Corinthians 15:3–4 for a summary of the gospel.
   c. Though hell is a real place, it may not be a "lake of fire." (It's not a problem if you think it is.) According to verse 9, what makes the fate of the wicked so painful?
   d. Can you describe an experience when you were separated from someone you loved?

5. 2 Peter 3:8–9. Why hasn't the Lord returned sooner? What is God's desire for everyone?

6. Matthew 6:19–21; Luke 16:8–9. Though we are not saved by works, what are you doing to prepare for eternity?

Doctrinal (Optional)

7. Philippians 3:19; 2 Peter 3:7. Is it possible these verses as well as others refer to the total destruction of the wicked? Why or why not?

8. Matthew 25:46. Why is Jesus' statement problematic for annihilationism?

Memory Verse: Revelation 14:13

Flesh

The word translated "flesh" (*sarx*) is used literally and metaphorically in the New Testament. When used literally, it refers to the physical substance that makes us human. In this sense *flesh* can refer to individuals or people corporately. As a metaphor, *flesh* refers to the human nature that is both susceptible to sin and sinful.

Study Questions

Flesh (Corporate)

1. Luke 3:6. The word translated "people" (NIV) is literally *flesh*. How was this prophecy fulfilled by Christ's life, death, and resurrection?

2. Acts 2:17. As above, the NIV has translated the word *flesh* as "people." Why is this promise significant for people who are not Jews?

Flesh (Individual)

3. 1 Corinthians 15:39, 50–56. Why can't "flesh and blood" inherit the kingdom of God? What will happen to our bodies of flesh so that we can live with God forever? How does knowing that your physical body (flesh) will be wonderfully transformed help you to cope with physical infirmities?

4. John 17:2. Again, *flesh* has been translated "people" (NIV). Why was Christ given "authority over all flesh (people)"? How does realizing that you have been chosen for eternal life motivate you to obedience in your Christian faith?

5. John 1:14. Why does John use the word *flesh* to refer to the incarnation (Jesus becoming a man)? What does the truth

that Jesus became "flesh" (made of the same stuff as our humanity) imply about the love of God (John 3:16)?

Optional

6. Though there were no gender controversies in the first century, what would have been some of the problems if John had written, "And the Word became a man . . . ?"

Flesh (Figure of Speech)

7. John 6:51–60. Jesus uses "eating his flesh" and "drinking his blood" as graphic figures of speech for belief. Why did many complain this was a "hard teaching," and desert Jesus (John 6:60, 66)? Why is it hard (difficult) for people to believe in Jesus today?

Flesh (Metaphorical)

8. Romans 7:5; 8:3–8. Why was the Law unable to save people, and why are we unable to save ourselves? Why does everyone need a Savior?

9. Romans 8:9–13. What happened to our "flesh" because we have trusted Christ as Savior? How does this help you to resist temptation?

10. Galatians 5:13, 16–23. Why is it important to realize that the "flesh" is the source of sin? What are the "acts of the flesh" (v. 19)? How can we walk daily in the power of the Spirit?

Optional

11. 1 Corinthians 15:44. Why does Paul say that our "body" (*soma*) not our "flesh" (*sarx*) will be transformed and raised from the dead?

Memory Verse: Galatians 5:16–17

Glorification

The ultimate destiny of all true believers is glorification. Jesus' last will and testament was for the restoration of the glory that he shared with his Father before he became a man and that believers would see the Son in all his glory (John 17:1–5, 22–24). Paul echoes Jesus' hope when he writes that because we are heirs with Christ we will be glorified with him (Romans 8:17). In the same chapter, he lists glorification as the last stage of redemption, "And those he predestined, he also called; those he called, he also justified; those he justified, he also glorified" (Romans 8:30).

Glory is difficult to define. It is technically not an attribute of God; rather it is the visible manifestation of all of his invisible attributes. What glorification means for us as believers is that we will receive a resurrection body that will be magnificent in appearance, perfect, powerful, and eternal (1 Corinthians 15:42–58). Paul says this amazing transformation will take place when Christ returns, the last trumpet sounds, and death is "swallowed up in victory" (1 Corinthians 15:51–57).

Study Questions

1. 1 Corinthians 15:42–44.
    a. How does Paul describe the resurrection body?
    b. How does this passage give hope to those who are physically challenged?

2. 1 Thessalonians 4:13–18. In this passage Paul writes to comfort those whose family members or friends have died.
    a. Grief is a normal response to the death of a loved one. Why does Paul say we should not grieve like unbelievers?

b. What does Paul say will happen when Christ returns?

c. According to verse 18, what is the purpose of Paul's teaching about the return of Christ? How would you use this passage to encourage someone who was grieving over the death of a loved one?

3. 1 Corinthians 15:50. Why do we need a resurrection body?

4. Philippians 1:20–21. Why is death gain for believers?

5. 1 John 3:2–3. What kind of resurrection body will we have if our resurrection body will be like Jesus' resurrection body? Because we have this hope, what does John say we should do (verse 3)?

Optional

6. Why is it important to believe in a real, physical resurrection body rather than only a spiritual body as some do (1 Corinthians 15:44)?

7. One of the paradoxical aspects of Jesus' life is that the path to glory was through suffering and death (John 17:4–5). Paul says the same is true for believers, "For our light and momentary troubles are achieving for us an eternal glory that far outweighs them all" (2 Corinthians 4:17). How does the hope of glory help you to cope with the inevitable pain and suffering of this life?

8. 1 Corinthians 15:51–57. Why do we fear death?

Memory Verse: 1 Corinthians 15:51–52

86

Grace

None of us have had a Damascus road experience like Paul. Believing that Jews who had become Christians were traitors, Paul was determined to wipe out Christianity. He was on his way to Damascus when he was knocked to the ground and blinded by a brilliant light. The light was the glory of Christ, who was not dead, but alive. There on his knees, Paul first experienced the amazing grace of God. Saul, the Jewish zealot, became Paul, the Christian apostle to the Gentiles (Acts 9:1–9).

This popular definition of grace is easy to remember:

God's
Riches
At
Christ's
Expense

Grace, "the unmerited favor" of God, is one of the fundamental truths that distinguishes Christianity from all other religions or religious cults. Like the Judaizers, who opposed Paul in the first century, religious teachers today claim we are saved by merit. According to them, we must do something to earn our salvation (Acts 15:1–2).

Grace oozes from the New Testament. Jesus taught about grace in the parable of the workers in the vineyard (Matthew 20:1–16). The early church was sustained by God's grace (Acts 4:33). Paul was willing to endure hardships, persecution, and even death because of God's grace (Acts 20:24). Paul insisted that any message that added anything to salvation by grace was not the "gospel"

(Galatians 1:6–7). Paul's classic statement about God's grace is in Ephesians 2:8–9: "For it is by grace you have been saved, through faith—and this is not from yourselves, it is the gift of God—not by works. . . ." Peter encourages believers to grow in grace (2 Peter 3:18), and refers to the Lord as "the God of all grace" (1 Peter 5:10). It is because of grace that Christ "taste[d] death for everyone," says the writer to the Hebrews (Hebrews 2:9). Jude says false teachers have perverted God's grace, using it as an excuse for immorality (Jude 4). Even John, who emphasizes primarily the love of God in his writings, marvels at the limitless grace of God revealed in Christ Jesus. He compares it to the waves of the ocean endlessly flowing over life (John 1:16), and he concludes Revelation with a benediction of God's grace (Revelation 22:21).

Study Questions

1. Ephesians 2:8–10. How would you explain the relationship between grace and works to a person who believes you must earn your salvation?
2. 1 Timothy 1:12–17. What would you say to a person who believes they are so bad that God would never save them?
3. Acts 20:22–24. If you're like me you probably go about your daily routine without thinking about God's grace. How can grace help us in our daily lives, especially when we face difficulties?
4. Acts 20:32. What is "the word [message] of grace"? How can it build us up?
5. Matthew 20:1–16. Why wasn't it unfair to pay the workers who worked only one hour as much as those who worked all day? How is this an example of grace?
6. Mark 10:23–27. How would you answer the disciples' question, "Who then can be saved?"

7. Titus 3:3–8. How has your life been changed because of God's grace?

8. 2 Peter 3:18. What does it mean to grow in grace? How can we do it?

9. John 1:14. How was Jesus' death on the cross a demonstration of God's grace?

10. Colossians 4:18. Paul ends almost all of his epistles with a salutation that includes "grace." How would this have been encouraging to the recipients, and how is this reminder of God's grace encouraging to us today?

Memory Verse: Acts 20:24 (Author's favorite verse)

87

Grief and Grieving

I vividly remember the first time I experienced deep, heartfelt grief. I was ten when I got Tiger. He was a puppy, and I cared for him like a mother. We grew together and bonded as only a boy and his dog can. I loved Tiger. One day when I came home from school I was met by a neighbor who said, "I have bad news. I think your dog was hit by a car and crawled under another car parked on the street." When I pulled Tiger from under the car, he was dead. Tears welled in my eyes, and I thought my heart was going to burst.

Severe emotional distress (grief) is inevitable in a world damaged by sin. Biblical writers describe a variety of circumstances that cause emotional pain. God created a perfect world (Genesis 1:31), but his heart was broken when he saw how wicked the world had become (Genesis 6:5–8). The book of Psalms is filled with the painful emotional experiences of failure, danger, disappointment, betrayal, disease, and death. For example, the psalmist laments, "My soul is weary with sorrow" (119:28). Isaiah describes the Messiah as a man of sorrows: "He was despised and rejected—a man of sorrows, acquainted with deepest grief" (53:3 NLT). Jesus wept at the tomb of Lazarus (John 11:35). Jesus warned that his followers should expect grief in a hostile world (John 16:22). The Thessalonians grieved for family and friends who had died (1 Thessalonians 4:13). Paul's relationship with the Corinthians caused him and the Corinthians severe pain (2 Corinthians 2:1–4, 7:8–10). The good news is that God will one day wipe away all of our tears (Revelation 21:4).

Study Questions

1. What are the various causes of grief according to the following passages?
   a. John 11:35; 1 Thessalonians 4:13
   b. John 16:20
   c. 1 Corinthians 5:1–2
   d. 2 Corinthians 2:1–4
   e. 2 Corinthians 6:3–13
   f. 1 Timothy 6:10
   g. Hebrews 12:11
   h. 1 Peter 1:6

2. What truth would you use from each of the following passages to comfort a person who is grieving over the loss of a family member or close friend?
   a. 1 Corinthians 15:50–58
   b. 2 Corinthians 5:1–5
   c. 1 Thessalonians 4:13–18

3. Hebrews 12:4–13. What is God's loving purpose in divine discipline? Though not necessarily discipline, how have painful circumstances helped you grow as a Christian?

4. 2 Corinthians 7:5–7. Why is it important to assure a grieving person that not only does God care but we do as well?

5. Ephesians 3:14–19. Why is it important that we pray for those who are grieving because of a painful loss?

Optional

6. Ephesians 4:30. What are some of the ways we can "grieve the Holy Spirit"? What does Paul encourage us to do in 4:31–32? What attitude changes do you need to make?

7. 2 Corinthians 4:16–18. Why is it important to view our present troubles in light of eternity?

Memory Verse: Revelation 21:4

Justification

In biblical usage, *justification* is a legal (forensic) term, primarily meaning "to declare righteous." It is a crucial part of Paul's message in the epistle to the Romans and is closely connected to *righteousness*. Paul concludes his argument that all (Gentiles and Jews) are sinful and in desperate need of God's righteousness in 3:9–20, and then he gives God's solution to the human predicament in 3:21–31. He is emphatic that no one can justify himself and no one is justified through keeping the Law. A person can only be put right with God by God himself. God justifies (declares not guilty) those who trust in Christ as Savior, and he will never demand that we pay the penalty for our sins.

But justification means more than believers are pardoned sinners. As our sin was imputed (transferred) to Christ, so Christ's righteousness was imputed to us, so we are actually righteous before God (Romans 3:22). Years ago I heard a helpful explanation by a theologian who said something like this: "If justification is only a pardon—that will keep us out of hell but not get us to heaven. We need Christ's righteousness to live with God forever."

Study Questions

1. Romans 5:15–17. What is the solution for the problem of sin? What is the reason why God can justify the guilty?

2. Romans 4:1–8. What two Old Testament persons did Paul use to support his argument that people are not justified by works? Why is it encouraging to know that you are not justified because of what you have done but because of your faith in what Christ has done for you?

3. Romans 5:18–19. Though some claim these verses teach universalism (the ultimate salvation of everyone), what does Paul write in verse 17 and Romans 3:26 that refutes universalism?

4. Romans 8:28–30. In verse 30, what does Paul say is the future hope for those who have been justified? How does this encourage you to live more like Christ?

5. 1 Corinthians 1:30; Philippians 3:9. In addition to a declaration of not guilty, what does Paul say we have received because of our faith in Christ?

6. Romans 8:33–34. What would you say to the person who thinks their misfortune is punishment for sins they have committed?

7. Romans 8:33–39. Why is Paul confident that nothing can ever reverse God's decision to justify us? How does this motivate you to be more like Christ?

8. Romans 5:1. What does Paul say is one result of our being justified? *The NLT Study Bible* says that this refers to more than "a mere feeling of peacefulness but to a real situation of peace."* What does it mean to know that you are no longer an enemy of God but at peace with him?

9. James 2:20–24. James's statement that "a person is considered righteous by what they do and not by faith alone" seems contradictory to Paul's insistence in Romans 3:20 that "no one will be declared righteous in God's sight by the works of the law." The resolution comes from recognizing that James is emphasizing how believers show to others that they have been justified and not how a person is justified by God. Paul would agree. He says that "good works" are the result of salvation by faith (Ephesians

* *The NLT Illustrated Study Bible* (Carol Stream, IL: Tyndale, 2015), 2053.

2:8–10). What is one specific way you can show others you have been justified? (See "Faith without Works Is Dead.")

Memory Verse: Romans 3:22–24

89

Lord's Day

SATURDAY OR SUNDAY?

The expression "the Lord's Day" occurs only in Revelation 1:10. John says that "on the Lord's Day" he was "in the Spirit" when he received a revelation from Jesus Christ. The expression could refer either to Sunday, the day the early church met for worship, or the day John received the revelation. The latter is more likely in my opinion, but many interpreters think it was Sunday.

Jesus was not a renegade Jew. As required by the law of Moses, he attended the synagogue regularly on the Sabbath (Luke 4:16). On several occasions, Jesus even taught in the synagogue on the Sabbath (Luke 6:6; 13:10). Because Jesus' disciples and the first Christians were Jews, it was only natural for them to continue to meet on the Sabbath (Saturday). Initially, the Jewish church apparently met daily: "Every day they continued to meet together in the temple courts" (Acts 2:46). The apostle Paul taught in the synagogue on the Sabbath (Acts 13:15–16).

Though some, such as Seventh Day Adventists, still insist on meeting on the Sabbath (Saturday), the church began meeting on Sunday early in its history. The church at Troas was meeting on Sunday when Paul visited them on his way to Jerusalem: "On the first day of the week we came together to break bread" (Acts 20:7). Paul admonished the church at Corinth to take up a collection for the poor on the first day of the week (1 Corinthians 16:2). The primary reason for meeting on Sunday was to honor the day Jesus rose from the dead. Plus, the church transitioned to Sunday to accommodate Gentiles, who did not observe the Sabbath.

Though from the first century the church has traditionally met on Sunday, the New Testament does not specifically prescribe a day for the gathering of believers. Rather, it describes what activities should be included when the church meets.

Study Questions

When does your church meet, and what are its practices? What do the following passages teach about the activities of the church?

1. Acts 2:42–47. This is the first of two descriptions of the church in Acts. Which of these activities should we practice in our churches today, and how does your church practice them?

2. Acts 20:7–12. In contrast to the church at Jerusalem, the church at Troas was Gentile. Was the meeting formal or informal? Where and when did they meet? What day? What time of day? What were their activities? What features, if any, should we practice in our churches today?

3. Colossians 3:16. The message or words of Christ are what was spoken by the Lord and the meaning of his teaching as recorded in the Epistles. How does your church practice what Paul has taught in this passage?

4. 1 Corinthians 11:23–26. What is the primary purpose of the Lord's Supper (Communion)? How often does your church celebrate Communion, and how can you keep it from becoming a meaningless ritual? What do you do to prepare yourself for Communion?

5. 1 Corinthians 16:1–2; 2 Corinthians 8:1–7. Why and to what extent should churches share their resources to help others? What is your church's strategy for helping individuals and other churches?

6. Revelation 1:10; John 4:23–24. What does it mean to worship God in Spirit and in truth? How does your church encourage meaningful worship? What do you do to foster authentic worship?

Memory Verse: Colossians 3:16

Reconciliation

A basic definition of reconciliation is the making of peace between two hostile parties. Paul teaches that because of humanity's rebellion, not only men and women but even nature itself is in a state of hostility with God (2 Corinthians 5:19; Colossians 1:20). Biblical reconciliation refers to removing this hostility, so that rebellious human beings are no longer enemies of God but friends. Paul writes in Ephesians that those who trust in Christ as Savior are no longer objects of God's wrath; instead they are children of God (2:1–5).

The New Testament presents Christ's sacrificial death and resurrection as the basis for reconciliation (2 Corinthians 5:21) and focuses on three dimensions of reconciliation. The most theologically important is the reconciliation of rebellious men and women with God (2 Corinthians 5:19). The second is the restoration of all creation (Romans 8:19–21; Colossians 1:20), and the third is establishing peace between hostile parties, especially Jews and Gentiles (Ephesians 2:14–16).

Study Questions

1. 2 Corinthians 5:18–21. This passage gives Paul's most extensive teaching on reconciliation.
   a. Who initiates the making of peace between man and God? Why do you think this is important?
   b. Who has God entrusted with the message of reconciliation? How will this change the way you relate to unbelievers?

c. What happened to those who know Christ (v. 17)? What are some of the changes of being a new person in Christ?
d. What specific aspect of Christ's sacrificial death makes possible reconciliation with God? The view that Christ's death was a substitutionary sacrifice for sin is commonly referred to as "vicarious atonement." How could one person (Christ) become a sacrifice for the whole world?
e. What aspect of Christ's human nature made it possible for him to become a sacrifice for sin? Why do you think this is important?

2. Colossians 1:21–22. What was it that made us enemies of God? What is our new relationship with God because of the reconciling work of Christ?

3. Colossians 2:9–10. What is the implication of Paul's statement about the nature of Christ's person? What is significant about the extent of our salvation (reconciliation) because of our union with Christ? Why would this matter if someone doubted or questioned the sufficiency of their salvation?

4. Romans 8:18–21. Paul reveals that all creation has been corrupted by sin but that God will one day fully restore everything. What are some examples of how nature has become an enemy of humanity? How does the miracle recorded in Mark 4:35–41 anticipate the reconciliation of nature?

5. Ephesians 2:14–16. What two groups of people were hostile but then reconciled to one another by Christ's death? What was the wall of hostility that separated the two groups? What are some of the walls that separate believers today? What are some ways to overcome one wall of hostility?

6. 2 Corinthians 2:5–11. Someone in the church at Corinth apparently had offended Paul and the Corinthians. Paul had written instructing the church to discipline him, which they had done, and the man had repented (sought forgiveness). Paul had forgiven him, but the Corinthians hadn't. What aspect of their salvation were they ignoring? Is there anyone you need to forgive (seek reconciliation)? How does this study on reconciliation help you to make peace with others?

Memory Verse: 2 Corinthians 5:18

91

Resurrection of Believers

The hope for the resurrection is not clear in the Old Testament. It is explicit in only one Old Testament passage. Michael, the archangel, promises Daniel that he will be resurrected with the righteous and that the unrighteous will be resurrected to everlasting shame (Daniel 12:1–3, 13). Note: There is a debate on whether or not Job expects to see God after death or before he dies (Job 19:25–26).

It is in the New Testament that we have overwhelming testimony about the resurrection. The two primary questions in the New Testament are about the nature of the resurrection body and the time of the resurrection.

Study Questions

1. John 11:21–26. When did Martha believe Lazarus would rise from the dead? What did Jesus mean when he said, "Whoever lives by believing in me will never die"?
2. 1 Corinthians 15:20–58. First Corinthians 15 is considered the most important chapter in the Bible on the resurrection. The Corinthians believed in the immortality of the soul but not the body. In the chapter, Paul attempts to explain the nature of the resurrection body.
   a. 1 Corinthians 15:20–24. What is the basis of our hope for a resurrection?
   b. 1 Corinthians 15:35–42. What are the analogies Paul uses to describe the resurrection body? To what extent will our resurrection bodies look like our current bodies? What will your grandparents look like?

   c. 1 Corinthians 15:50. Why do we need a resurrection body? What are some of the physical problems we experience that remind us we will need a new body to inherit the kingdom of God?
   d. 1 Corinthians 15:51–53. When will we receive our resurrection bodies? Philippians 1:21–23. What will happen when we die?
   e. 1 Corinthians 15:58. How does the hope of the resurrection motivate you to live for Christ and serve him?

3. 2 Corinthians 5:1–5.
   a. In addition to the resurrection of Christ, what has God given us as a guarantee of the resurrection?
   b. What life experiences cause you to look forward to a new heavenly body?

4. 1 Thessalonians 4:13–18. How do you respond to the death of a family member or close friend?

5. Revelation 21:3–4. What are some of the painful memories that will be gone forever in heaven?

—Optional

6. 1 Corinthians 15:50. Do you think the New Testament evidence supports a physical or spiritual resurrection body?

Memory Verse: John 11:25–26

92

Righteousness

Righteousness is not a word that is used much today, but it is used abundantly in both the Old and New Testaments. When John resisted Jesus' request for baptism, Jesus replied, "It is proper for us to do this to fulfill all righteousness" (Matthew 3:15). In his inaugural address, Jesus emphasized righteousness rather than keeping the Law by saying, "Blessed are those who hunger and thirst for righteousness" (Matthew 5:6). His message was even more countercultural when he said, "Unless your righteousness exceeds that of the scribes and Pharisees, you will never enter into the kingdom of heaven" (Matthew 5:20 ESV). Later in the same message, Jesus said, "Seek first his kingdom and his righteousness and all these things will be given to you as well" (Matthew 6:33). According to Luke, the centurion who witnessed the crucifixion testified about Jesus, "Surely this was a righteous man" (Luke 23:47). Jesus promised his disciples that when the Holy Spirit came, he would convict the world "about sin and righteousness and judgment" (John 16:8).

When Paul presented the gospel to the Roman governor Felix, he spoke about "righteousness, self-control, and the judgment" (Acts 24:25). The theme of Paul's magnificent epistle to the Romans is "the righteousness of God" (Romans 1:17). To argue that salvation has always been by faith and not the works of the Law, Paul quotes Genesis 15:6: "So Abraham 'believed God, and it was credited to him as righteousness'" (Galatians 3:6). James warned that "anger does not produce the righteousness that God desires" (James 1:20). Peter refers to Noah as a "preacher of righteousness" and Lot as a "righteous man" (2 Peter 2:5, 7). He encourages those who were threatened by false teachers to look forward to "a new heaven and a new earth, where righteousness dwells" (2 Peter 3:13).

John describes a multitude worshiping in heaven clothed in their "righteous deeds" (Revelation 19:8 ESV).

Righteousness or *righteous* means "what is right." The best modern equivalent is the term *justice* or *just*. Righteousness is a moral attribute (characteristic) of God (Romans 1:17), making him the ultimate standard of what is right and motivating him to bring those who put their faith in Christ into a right relationship with him and to judge those who reject Christ. Because Jesus was God incarnate, he was the perfect embodiment of righteousness (1 John 2:1), thus God grants his righteousness to those who put their faith in Christ (Romans 3:22–24).

Study Questions

1. Romans 3:25–26. Paul states that God demonstrates his righteous justice by justifying ("declaring just") those who put their faith in his Son. Why is it fair (just) for God to justify those who trust Christ as Savior and to judge those who refuse Christ?
2. Philippians 3:7–11. How has your life changed since you became a believer?
3. Romans 1:16–17. How is the righteousness of God revealed in the gospel?
4. Romans 1:18–20. Why does everyone need God's righteousness?
5. John 16:7–11. What did Jesus mean when he said the Spirit would convict the world about righteousness?
6. Matthew 5:6, 20; 6:33. In the Sermon on the Mount do you think Jesus was teaching about lifestyle righteousness or forensic righteousness (a right standing before God)? Why? Do you think it is possible that Jesus was teaching about both?

7. 1 John 1:8–9. Most commentators agree that this passage is for those who are already believers. What is the basis for God's forgiveness (see 1 John 2:1–2)?

8. 1 Peter 2:24. What does Peter say has happened to Christ on the cross that enables us to live righteously?

9. 2 Corinthians 5:21. What are two aspects of God's saving actions that make it possible for us to be right with him?

Memory Verse: Romans 3:22–24

93

Sanctification

A prominent theologian stated that it is hard to imagine anyone would argue that because grace has canceled out our sin we should go on sinning so that God can show us more of his amazing grace.* But that's exactly the twisted thinking Paul refutes in Romans 6. Paul asks the hypothetical question, "Shall we go on sinning so that grace may increase?" (Romans 6:1). His answer is abrupt, "Absolutely not!" (Romans 6:2 CSB). Paul then explains the process of becoming free from sin and more like Christ (Romans 6:2–23). This progressive transformation in the life of a believer is called sanctification.

Unlike *justification*, which refers to the immediate change in our legal standing when we trust Christ as Savior, *sanctification* refers to the lifelong process of becoming more like Christ. God justifies us by his grace. We do not justify ourselves. But we are active participants in sanctification, working together with God to complete our salvation (Philippians 2:12–13).

Though from God's perspective we are both justified and sanctified at the moment of salvation (1 Corinthians 1:2), sanctification is the process of becoming in practice what we are positionally in Christ. Some believe that we can attain sinless perfection in this life, but Scripture seems to support the view that we will not be completely free from sin until we are glorified (Romans 8:28–30). I have found the following comparison helpful:

Justification—Free from the penalty of sin
Sanctification—Free from the power of sin
Glorification—Free from the presence of sin

* I. Howard Marshall, *New Testament Theology* (Downers Grove, IL: InterVarsity, 2004), 316.

Study Questions

1. Romans 6:6–7. What has happened to believers so that we are no longer slaves to sin?
2. Romans 6:11–14.
   a. What are the practical steps Paul gives for overcoming the power of sin? You can identify them with the verbs in the verses.
   b. What does it mean to "count yourselves dead to sin"?
3. Romans 6:15–23.
   a. What is the extended illustration Paul uses in this passage to describe our new status in Christ?
   b. What does it mean to be a slave to righteousness?
   c. How does this motivate you to obey God and not let sin be your master?
   d. According to 6:22–23, what are the contrasting consequences of obedience to God and slavery to sin?
4. Philippians 2:12–13. In these verses we see that sanctification involves both human effort and divine enablement.
   a. What does it mean "to work out your salvation"? Note the difference between "working for your salvation" and "working out your salvation."
   b. How is God working in us to accomplish "his good purpose"?
5. 1 John 3:1–3.
   a. Why does John say we should make every effort to keep ourselves pure?
   b. What is the imagery that John uses to describe believers?
   c. What does this suggest about the completion of the process of sanctification?

d. How does knowing that you are destined to be like Christ motivate you to be more like Christ now?

Memory Verse: Romans 6:11–12

94

Savior

A TITLE OF CHRIST

The angel told Joseph to name his son Jesus, "because he will save his people from their sins" (Matthew 1:21). *Savior* means "deliverer." In the Old Testament God is the ultimate and only deliverer of his people (Isaiah 43:11–13); however, the prophets looked forward to the coming of the Messiah (Servant), who would save all people (Isaiah 49:6, 8).

In the New Testament Jesus is the Savior (Luke 2:11). He does not replace God as Savior but is sent by God to save the world (John 3:16–17). In the Gospels and Acts the title *Savior* is not used often, but Jesus' mission is salvation. After talking to Jesus, the Samaritans concluded that he was indeed "the Savior of the world" (John 4:42). In Luke's Gospel, Jesus announced his mission was "to seek and to save the lost" (Luke 19:10). And Luke emphasizes that "the lost" includes everyone, especially the outcasts. Though the Jews were oppressed by the Romans, Jesus came to save people from a greater threat—their sins (Matthew 1:21).

Paul refers to Christ as "Savior" in Ephesians 5:23 and Philippians 3:20, but his most frequent use of the title *Savior* is in the Pastorals (1 & 2 Timothy and Titus). Note that Jesus shares the same title and function as God.

Study Questions

1. What does the alternation between God and Christ in the following passages imply about the person and mission of Jesus Christ?
    a. God—1 Timothy 1:1; 2:3; 4:10; Titus 1:3; 2:10; 3:4
    b. Christ—2 Timothy 1:10; Titus 1:4; 2:13; 3:6

2. 1 Timothy 2:1–3. Why should we pray for all people? How do we pray for cruel tyrants or for those with different political views?

3. Titus 2:13. This is a remarkable statement. Jesus is actually called God. Why does it matter if Jesus were actually God or only became God?

4. Titus 2:11–14. This passage gives us one of the unique features of the Pastoral Epistles. The incarnation (the coming of Jesus in the flesh) is called an "epiphany."
   a. What can we learn for godly living from the grace of God that appeared in the coming of Christ?
   b. What is "the blessed hope"? If you are really looking forward to the return of Christ, how are you preparing yourself for his glorious and great appearing?

5. In addition to the Pastorals, *Savior* is used five times in 2 Peter (1:1, 11; 2:20; 3:2, 18) and once in 1 John 4:14 and Jude 25.
   a. 2 Peter 2:20. Why are people who have escaped the wickedness of the world and then returned to it worse off than if they had never known the truth of the gospel?
   b. 1 John 4:14–16. How do we know that God loves us? If we live in God and God lives in us, *How Then Should We Live?*
   c. Jude 25. What are three references in Jude's wonderful doxology that you can use to praise God the next time you pray?

Memory Verse: 1 Timothy 2:3

95

Scripture

Scripture! When we hear that term, most of us think of the Bible. Throughout history Christians have equated the thirty-nine books of the Old Testament and the twenty-seven books of the New Testament with Scripture. However, the Bible of Jesus and the early church was the Old Testament.

The word *Scripture* is a translation of the Greek word *graphe*, which means "the writings." It occurs fifty-one times in the New Testament. In the parable of the tenants, Jesus referred to Psalm 118:22–23 as "the Scriptures" (Matthew 21:42). In his account of the two men on the road to Emmaus, Luke identifies the Old Testament as "the Scriptures": "And beginning with Moses and all the Prophets, he explained to them what was said in all the Scriptures concerning himself" (Luke 24:27). And when the two men recalled their "Emmaus Road" experience, they asked, "Were not our hearts burning within us while he talked with us on the road and opened the Scriptures to us?" (Luke 24:32). When the Sadducees tried to embarrass Jesus with a trick question about the resurrection, he faulted them for not knowing the Old Testament. He said, "You are in error because you do not know the Scriptures or the power of God" (Matthew 22:29).

Both Paul and Peter identified the Old Testament as *Scripture*. Paul assured Timothy that "all Scripture" was inspired (*theoneustos*, the very breath of God) (2 Timothy 3:16). Peter warns about believing the myths of false teachers and assures believers of the truth of Scripture: "Above all, you must understand that no prophecy of Scripture came about by the prophet's own interpretation of things. For prophecy never had its origin in the human will, but prophets, though human, spoke from God as they were carried along by the Holy Spirit" (2 Peter 1:20–21).

Though almost all uses of *Scripture* in the New Testament refer to the Old Testament or various parts of it, some identify parts of the New Testament as Scripture. Peter compares Paul's writings to Scripture when he says that "ignorant and unstable people distort" his writings "as they do the other Scriptures" (2 Peter 3:16). In 1 Timothy 5:18, Paul quotes from Jesus' words in Luke 10:7 and calls them "Scripture."

Study Questions

1. 2 Timothy 3:16. How would you explain to someone why you believe the Bible is the Word of God?
2. Revelation 22:18–19. Though the warning is specifically about the book of Revelation, do you think it could apply to the rest of the New Testament? How would you tactfully respond to someone who claims their group has other books that are from God?
3. Acts 1:16–20. How does Peter identify what David predicted about Judas? What does this imply about the Old Testament?
4. 1 Thessalonians 2:13. How did the Thessalonians accept Paul's preaching? What does this imply about Paul's writings in the New Testament?
5. 1 Corinthians 14:37. What did Paul believe about his teaching? How should we regard the teachings of Scripture today?
6. Psalm 12:6. If Scripture is the Word of God, should we believe and obey everything in it? Is there something you don't want to believe or obey?
7. 2 Peter 1:20–21. How would you answer a person who teaches something that is contradictory to the Bible?

8. John 16:12–15. What does Jesus promise his disciples? How would you answer a person who says because the Gospels and the other books of the New Testament were written at least thirty years after the life of Christ, they cannot possibly be accurate?

9. Luke 24:25–27. Why do some people find it hard to believe what's in the Bible? Is there anything in the Bible that you find hard to believe? Why?

10. Do you agree or disagree with the following statement: "What the Bible says is what God says"? Why?

Memory Verse: 2 Timothy 3:16

Sovereignty of God

A good friend of mine recently told me that his teaching position was being terminated at the end of the school year. I naturally asked, "What are you going to do?" He said he didn't know, but he was a Calvinist and was confident that God was in control. His answer reflects his understanding of God's sovereignty.

Sovereignty is God's infinite power and absolute control over creation. Though God's sovereignty is revealed in the Old Testament, especially in the Psalms, the classic text is in the New Testament: "And we know that in all things God works for the good of those who love him, who have been called according to his purpose" (Romans 8:28).

"If God can do anything, can he make a rock so big that he cannot move it?" is a question often asked about God's sovereignty. The question comes from a misunderstanding of God's power and will. God can do anything, but what he does must be consistent with his character and will. For example, God cannot lie (Hebrews 6:18; Titus 1:2) because that would be inconsistent with his holy character. Nor can God be tempted, and he doesn't tempt people because that too would violate his holiness (James 1:13).

The major question, however, for most of us is not about what God can or cannot do but why. As I write this the most devastating wildfires in recent history are burning out of control in California. Thousands and thousands of acres have burned, and there have been billions of dollars in property loss. In addition to natural disasters, we are all affected by misfortune and disease. "If God is all powerful," we ask, "why does he allow these sorts of things to happen?"

Study Questions

1. Romans 8:28.
   a. How would you comfort a person who has just been diagnosed with cancer?
   b. What would you say to a person who has lost everything, including their home, in a fire?
2. Luke 13:34–33. How does Jesus' statement indicate confidence in God's sovereignty? Do you think God can use the evil intentions of people to accomplish his purposes? How does this affect the way you think about situations where people have taken advantage of you?
3. Genesis 50:19–21.
   a. What did Joseph believe about God's purposes in his brothers' selling him as a slave? Can you recall a situation where another person intended to harm you but God used it for good?
   b. Do you think Joseph realized that God was in control when his brothers sold him into slavery? If you have experienced misfortune, what made you aware of God's sovereignty over your circumstances?
4. Romans 8:28–30. The views on this passage form a theological divide between Calvinists and Arminians. The former believe that God chooses some for salvation but rejects others. The latter believe that God chooses those he foreknew would believe. What is the relationship between God's sovereignty and human freedom in the matter of salvation? (Tough question!)
5. Acts 18:18–22. What did Paul tell the Ephesians who wanted him to spend more time with them? What is the relationship between our personal plans and God's sovereignty?

6. Acts 2:22–24. Do you think it was fair for Peter to charge that the Jews and "wicked men" were responsible for the death of Jesus? (Another tough question!)
7. 1 Thessalonians 2:18. Paul tells the Thessalonians that he wanted to return to see them but was prevented by Satan. How would you explain what Paul wanted to do, Satan's opposition, and God's sovereignty?

Memory Verse: Romans 8:28

97

Spiritual Gifts

One of the Spirit's ministries is the giving of gifts to equip believers for ministry (1 Corinthians 12:7). A spiritual gift is a special ability given and empowered by the Holy Spirit for ministry in the church. Though gifts are given by the same Holy Spirit, gifts vary. No one has all the gifts, but every believer has at least one gift (1 Corinthians 12:7).

Spiritual gifts are listed in only two passages—1 Corinthians 12 and Romans 12. Miraculous gifts are listed in 1 Corinthians, but not in Romans. Paul refers to apostles, prophets, evangelists, and pastor-teachers in Ephesians 4:11, but I think these are offices or ministries rather than gifts. Peter encourages believers to serve faithfully with whatever gift they have received but doesn't identify specific gifts (1 Peter 4:11).

Study Questions

1. John 14:16–17; Acts 2:1–4; 1 Corinthians 12:7. What is the difference between the gift of the Spirit and the gifts of the Spirit? When does a person receive the gift of the Spirit (see Titus 3:5)?
2. 1 Corinthians 12:7–12.
   a. What is the purpose of spiritual gifts?
   b. Should churches encourage believers to discover and use their spiritual gifts? What are some of the advantages and disadvantages of doing this?
   c. Do you know your gift? How do you use it?

3. 1 Corinthians 12:12–26; Romans 12:4–5.
   a. What is the analogy that Paul uses to explain spiritual gifts?
   b. Why is this a helpful analogy for describing spiritual gifts?

4. Romans 12:6–8. The gifts Paul lists in Romans is different than in 1 Corinthians. One notable difference is that there are no supernatural gifts listed in Romans 12. This has led many to conclude the two lists are only representative and not comprehensive.
   a. Do you think there are gifts other than those listed in Scripture?
   b. Do you think people can have more than one spiritual gift at the same time?
   c. Do you think spiritual gifts are permanent, or can a person's gift change according to the needs of the church or the circumstances of the individual?

5. Romans 12:3–5.
   a. What is the problem that Paul is addressing in the church at Rome?
   b. And how does his teaching on spiritual gifts address this problem?
   c. Do you think teaching about spiritual gifts is an effective way of encouraging people to serve, or can it create problems in a church?

6. 1 Corinthians 13:1–13; Romans 12:9–10. Why does Paul emphasize love as the single most important motivation for all Christian service?

Optional

The topic of spiritual gifts is confusing and controversial. Two reasons are as follows:

7. Because of the numerous questions about the discovery and use of gifts, some have suggested that spiritual gifts (*charismata*) are actually different Spirit-inspired ministries. This means that people should determine where they should serve based mainly on the needs of the church and their abilities and interests instead of spiritual gifts. If you have a ministry in the church, how did you decide on that ministry?

8. Many sincere and godly Christians believe in the continuation of the miraculous gifts of healing, speaking in tongues, prophecy (predicting the future), etc. Based on 1 Corinthians 13:8–13, others believe the miraculous gifts, and perhaps all of the gifts, have ceased with the completion of the canon of Scripture.

   Whatever view you and your church hold, what will last forever and when will we have a full understanding of the will of God?

Memory Verse: Romans 12:9–10

Trinity

Many believers are surprised to learn that the word *Trinity* is not found in the Bible. However, though the word is not used, the concept of the Trinity is clearly revealed in the New Testament. Simply put, orthodox Christians believe that one God exists eternally as the Father, Son, and Holy Spirit. Christians do not believe in three gods (tritheism) as some charge; Christians believe in one God (monotheism) who exists as three distinct persons.

The first hint of the Trinity is at the baptism of Jesus. God the Father speaks from heaven, "This is my beloved Son," and the Holy Spirit descends on Jesus in the form of a dove (Matthew 3:16–17 KJV). Jesus claimed unity with God when he said, "I and my Father are one" (John 10:30 KJV). In meeting with his disciples in an upper room, Jesus assured them that anyone who had seen him had seen the Father because he and the Father were one and the same (John 14:9–11). He also promised to send them "another advocate" (the Holy Spirit) (John 14:16). The Greek term for "another" is *allos,* which means another of the same kind, with the implication that Jesus and the Holy Spirit are one and the same. In the Great Commission, Jesus told his followers to make disciples of all nations, "baptizing them in the name of the Father and of the Son and of the Holy Spirit" (Matthew 28:19). "Name" is singular indicating unity, yet the use of the article with each of the persons upholds their distinction from one another.

The Trinity is also attested in the Epistles. Paul affirms there is only one God. He justifies people by faith (Romans 3:30), and he wants everyone to be saved (1 Timothy 2:4–5). Yet Paul declares that Jesus Christ is "our great God and Savior" (Titus 2:13). And he equates the Holy Spirit with God when he states that as no one can know the mind of a man except the man himself so no one can know the mind of God except the Spirit of God (1 Corinthians 2:10–12). Paul, however, recognizes that the Father, the Son, and the Holy Spirit are three distinct persons: "May the grace of the Lord Jesus Christ, and the love of God, and the fellowship of the Holy Spirit be with you all" (2 Corinthians 13:14).

Study Questions

1. John 20:28–29. Until Jesus appeared to Thomas and the other disciples, Thomas doubted that the Lord had risen from the dead. How does Thomas's response give proof for the deity of Christ? Why do you think Jesus said, "Blessed are those who have not seen and yet have believed"?
2. Acts 5:3–4. How does Peter's charge against Ananias support the deity of the Holy Spirit?
3. In the previous passage and Ephesians 4:30, what is the evidence that the Holy Spirit is a person and not a power?
4. Matthew 28:19. How would you answer the charge that Christians believe in three gods?
5. Jude 20–21. How does this passage reveal that the three persons of the Trinity are distinct from one another?
6. Ephesians 3:14–21. How does Paul's prayer reveal the unity and diversity of the Trinity? How does the concept of Trinity (unity in diversity) help foster respect and harmony between believers who are ethnically and culturally different?

Optional

Jehovah's Witnesses believe that Jesus was created as the Son of God. Their view is not new. Arius (AD 250–336), bishop at Alexandria, claimed that Jesus, the Son of God, was created and was not God from eternity. He taught that the Son and the Holy Spirit were only "similar" to God and not of the same "substance."

The church rejected the teaching of Arius and formulated the doctrine of the Trinity at the Council of Nicea in AD 325 and reaffirmed the creed at the Council of Constantinople in AD 381. Athanasius, who was later a bishop at Alexandria, was an early champion of the Trinity; and though he was viciously attacked by Arians, he devoted his life to defending the doctrine of the Trinity. "The Athanasian Creed" is still used by churches today as their doctrinal statement of the Trinity.

7. Ephesians 1:3–14. Why do you think it is important for us to believe that the Father, the Son, and the Holy Spirit are of the same essence (substance) and have existed from eternity as three distinct persons?

Memory Verse: Matthew 28:19–20

99

Union with Christ

Years ago, one of my theological mentors made a profound statement. He said, "If Christ loved us enough to die for us, he loves us enough to live in us." His comment reflects one of the remarkable miracles of faith: "We are in Christ, and he is in us." It is through this supernatural union with Christ that we receive all the benefits of salvation.

Paul cautions the arrogant Corinthians against foolishly boasting that they had somehow saved themselves. Rather he says they matter to God not because of who they are but because of who they are in Christ. "It is because of him that you are in Christ Jesus, who has become for us wisdom from God—that is, our righteousness, holiness and redemption. Therefore, as it is written: 'Let the one who boasts boast in the Lord'" (1 Corinthians 1:30–31). The work of the Spirit is crucial to this union with Christ. He baptizes believers into the body of Christ (1 Corinthians 12:13).

Our union with Christ is reciprocal. We are not only "in Christ," Jesus also lives in us through the indwelling Spirit (Ephesians 3:17; 2 Corinthians 3:17–18). While he was on earth, Jesus was with his followers, but after his resurrection and ascension, Jesus sent the Holy Spirit to dwell in believers (Acts 2:38). Paul boldly proclaims that anyone who does not have the Spirit does not have Christ because the Spirit of God is the Spirit of Christ (Romans 8:9).

Christ in us is a transforming and empowering union. The life we now live is not by human effort but by the supernatural power of Christ, who lives in us (Galatians 2:20).

We are not merely in Christ as individuals; we are one in Christ with other believers. Paul's favorite metaphor for this corporate unity is the body of Christ (Romans 12:5; 1 Corinthians 12:12–14). Though we may be different ethnically and culturally, we are one in Christ. "There is neither Jew nor Gentile, slave nor free, nor is there male and female, for you are all one in Christ" (Galatians 3:28).

Study Questions

1. Romans 8:9–11. Why does Paul say we have eternal life?
2. Galatians 2:20. How can you increase an awareness of Christ living in you in your daily life? Can you recall a specific event in which you sensed the power of Christ working through you?
3. Ephesians 1:3–6. In what ways is it encouraging to realize that God chose you to be "in Christ" before the creation of the world?
4. John 17:20–21. What was Jesus' prayer for those who would believe in him in the future? How does this affect your relationship with other believers, especially those who are different?
5. Philippians 3:7–11. How would you assess your former life in comparison to your union with Christ?
6. Ephesians 1:22. The Ephesians had been totally immersed in the occult prior to their conversion (Acts 19:11–20). Though they were now "in Christ" they were still terrified of demonic powers. In an incredible statement, Paul assures them that Christ is now in a position of authority over every evil power in the universe. What do you fear, and how does the knowledge that you are "in Christ" help you to overcome your fears?
7. 1 Corinthians 1:30. Which one of these benefits of our union with Christ is most meaningful to you and why?

8. Romans 6:1–4. Paul uses the illustration of baptism to describe the experience of becoming one with Christ in his death and resurrection as the motivating idea for overcoming sin. How will this help you in your efforts to sin less?

Memory Verse: Galatians 2:20

World

When I was in seminary years ago I was required to read a book by Harold Lindsell, *The World, the Flesh, and the Devil*. If I remember correctly, his point was that to avoid sinning we need to correctly identify the source of temptation. In this study we will focus on the world. *World* is a translation of several different Greek terms in the New Testament, but we will limit our study to the translation of *kosmos*, used over 180 times and the most significant term.

The term *world* (cosmos) is used in four ways:

1. As the totality of creation (everything) (Acts 17:24).
2. As the physical earth as the dwelling place of people (Matthew 4:8; Romans 1:8).
3. As the people who live in the world (John 17:21).
4. As a wicked, seductive, and doomed system (1 John 2:15–17).

Study Questions

As Creation

1. Acts 17:24–26. Paul was speaking to Epicurean and Stoic philosophers who didn't believe in a personal "god" who was the creator of everything and sustainer of life. What are two encouraging truths about God?

As the Planet Earth (the physical world)

2. Matthew 24:21; Hebrews 4:3. What is the implication about the origin of the earth?

As the Dwelling Place of People (Believers and Unbelievers)

3. Matthew 13:36–43. How does Jesus divide people in the world? What are some of the evidences that we live in the midst of weeds (evil people)? What happens at the end of the age?
4. 2 Peter 2:5. Who was protected when God destroyed the "world" with a flood? What is Peter's warning to unbelievers (2:9)? What is an effective way to warn unbelievers of divine judgment? Do you think people today will listen? Why or why not?
5. 1 Corinthians 4:9. *Kosmos* is translated "whole universe" in the NIV, and "entire world" in the NLT. How does knowing that angels are witnesses to events on earth make a difference in how you view life's circumstances?
6. John 15:18–21. What kind of hostility have you experienced that Jesus warns about in this passage? John 15:26–27. Though we may be persecuted, what is our responsibility to the world?

As a Wicked and Doomed System

7. 1 John 2:15–17.
   a. What three sources of temptation are identified in this passage?
   b. What are some of the specific temptations we face in these three areas?
   c. Though sin is appealing, what do we need to remember about the "world"?
8. John 16:33. How can we experience peace in an evil and hostile world?

Memory Verse: John 3:16; 2 Corinthians 5:19

Worry

"Why do anything when you can worry?" is the unspoken motto of many. We all worry. It is an age-old problem. Jesus spoke extensively about worry in the Sermon on the Mount (Matthew 6:25–34). The story of the sisters Mary and Martha is a classic contrast between a worrier and a devoted disciple who sits at the feet of Jesus (Luke 10:38–42). Paul reminds us that instead of worrying we should pray (Philippians 4:6–7).

What is worry? Worry is an emotional response to people and/or circumstances that at a minimum causes stress and at its worst is incapacitating. It is important to distinguish between legitimate concerns and unhealthy worry. In the Sermon on the Mount, Jesus makes three distinctions between worry and concerns (Matthew 6:25–34):

1. Jesus said, "Don't worry. Consider the birds and the flowers and how God cares for them. Aren't you more important? Don't you believe that God will provide for your needs?" People who worry trust in themselves. People with concerns trust in God.
2. People worry about matters they can't change: "Can any one of you by worrying add a single hour to your life?" (v. 27). People with concerns differentiate between circumstances they can and can't change, and they plan and act to do something about what they can change.
3. People who worry tend to think more about themselves than God's kingdom and how their circumstances can help advance the kingdom and develop Christlike character. "But seek first his kingdom and his righteousness, and all these things will be given to you as well" (v. 33).

4. To what Jesus said, I would like to add one more. It seems to me that Paul's concerns were about people, not things. One example: Paul changed his plans to preach at Troas because he was concerned about Titus. Instead of worrying he went to Macedonia to find him (2 Corinthians 2:12–13). Most of us worry about our possessions, not people.

None of us will enjoy the luxury of a problem-free life. Jesus warned, "In this world you will have trouble. But take heart! I have overcome the world" (John 16:33). Answer the following questions and "Don't worry. Be happy!"

Study Questions

1. John 16:33. How does your relationship with Christ make a difference in how you respond to everyday problems? To unexpected and sometimes traumatic circumstances?
2. Matthew 6:27. What are some of the current circumstances in your life that you can't change and some that you can change? What is your plan for coping with the circumstances you can change?
3. Matthew 6:34. What are some of the matters you worry about that have never happened and will probably never happen? What can you do to avoid worrying about them?
4. Luke 10:38–42.
    a. Do you identify more with Mary or Martha? Why?
    b. What did Jesus mean when he said, "Mary has chosen what is better"?
    c. How do you schedule your daily routine to spend time with the Lord?
    d. What is your greatest concern (worry) in life? What does this reveal about what is important to you?

5. Philippians 4:4–7.
   a. What is your first and typical response to a challenge or problem?
   b. What did Paul encourage us to do rather than worry?
   c. What can you do to develop a peaceful heart?

Memory Verse: Philippians 4:6–7

102

Wrath of God

Some might question teaching about the wrath of God because of the emphasis in the Bible on the love of God. But in both the Old and New Testaments, the writers describe the wrath of God against sin. For example, Moses describes God's wrath against Israel because of idolatry (Exodus 32:9–10). Zephaniah, the prophet, gives a vivid description of the pouring out of God's wrath on the whole earth in the day of judgment (1:2–3). After John tells that God sent his Son into the world because of his amazing love, he warns, "Whoever believes in the Son has eternal life, but whoever rejects the Son will not see life, for God's wrath remains on them" (John 3:36). Some of the strongest statements about the wrath of God are found in Paul's writings. Paul writes in Romans that not only is God revealing his righteousness but his wrath as well: "The wrath of God is being revealed from heaven against all the godlessness and wickedness of people, who suppress the truth by their wickedness" (1:18). He says such people are without excuse because they have deliberately rejected God (1:19–20). John describes the final judgments on the earth as "the great day of his wrath" (Revelation 6:17).

What is wrath? It is not how we sometimes respond to people. We, unfortunately, react with uncontrolled anger or rage when someone offends us. God does not. Wrath is God's controlled and just response to his anger at sin, and it is entirely accurate to classify it as an attribute of God. It is closely connected to divine justice. If God did not judge sin and sinners he would not be just.

Study Questions

1. John 3:16–18, 36. In witnessing, do you think we should tell unbelievers about both the love of God and the wrath of

God? Why or why not? How would you balance a message about the love of God and the wrath of God?

2. Romans 2:5–11. Paul is not teaching that salvation is by works rather than a gift of God; rather, he is contrasting a life that will end in destruction with one that ends with eternal life. How does this motivate you to live in holiness?

3. Colossians 3:5–12. Paul states that we must get rid of the practices of our old life because “the wrath of God” is coming, and put on the virtues of our new life in Christ.
   a. If we believe in eternal security, why does Paul warn of “the wrath of God” as a motivation for Christian living?
   b. What are the difficulties we have with getting rid of the habits of our old life and developing habits of our new life?

4. Romans 5:8–11. Paul is speaking here of the wrath to come.
   a. What is remarkable about the love of God?
   b. How has our relationship with God been changed?
   c. Do we need to fear God’s wrath on the day of judgment? Why not?

5. Psalm 103:8–9. What attribute of God is balanced with his wrath? Why should we be thankful for this attribute?

6. 2 Peter 3:9–10. Why hasn’t Christ returned sooner? Why should this motivate us for evangelism?

7. Psalm 4:4; Ephesians 4:26–27. Should we imitate God’s wrath (anger) against sin, and in what ways can we do this so we don’t sin?

Memory Verse: Ephesians 2:3–5

Acknowledgments

When I wrote this book I was in the process of making one of the biggest changes in my life. After teaching for thirty-seven years at Moody Bible Institute, I retired. For twenty-five years we lived only a short distance from the school in downtown Chicago. When I retired we moved to a small town in rural Colorado to be near our grandkids. The geography and culture were completely different. Plus, I went from a fast-paced and busy lifestyle to a snail's pace. It was a tough transition. I didn't know what to do with my time. I was bored.

Andy McGuire came to my rescue. He asked me to write two books—this one and a book of Jesus' parables. I want to thank him for his confidence and encouragement. He has richly blessed my life. The book was his idea. I also want to thank Ellen Chalifoux, who edited my academic style, corrected errors, and helped credit sources. She was tactful, courteous, and almost always right when she suggested changes. Her careful attention to detail was invaluable. My wife also deserves credit. In addition to coping with my moodiness, she read the studies, made suggestions to clarify the commentary and questions, and helped with proofreading.

God has blessed me far more than I deserve, and I thank him for his amazing grace, which he continues to pour out in my life in surprising ways.

About the Author

Dr. William H. Marty taught at Moody Bible Institute for thirty-seven years. His main emphasis was teaching an Old and New Testament survey to freshmen at the Chicago campus, and the fruit of his focus on teaching the story line of the Bible was published in *The Whole Bible Story*. Dr. Marty has also written *The World of Jesus* and *The Jesus Story* and coauthored *A Quick-Start Guide to the Whole Bible*. *The Whole Bible Story* has been published in Korean, and *The World of Jesus* has appeared in German, Arabic, and Hungarian. Bill lives in Colorado with his wife, Linda, and they have two children and two grandchildren. Bill is an active triathlete and has competed at the national and international levels.

More Foundational Biblical Resources

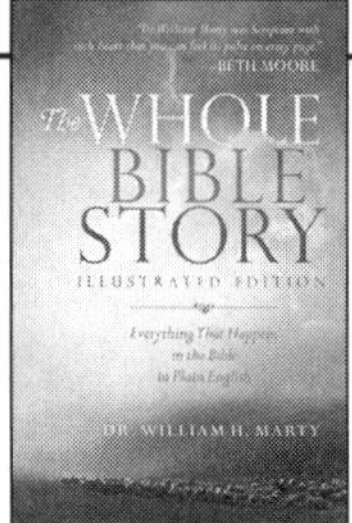

The sweeping narrative of the Bible presented in one engaging, easy-to-read story. Includes full-color maps and photos.

The Whole Bible Story by Dr. William H. Marty

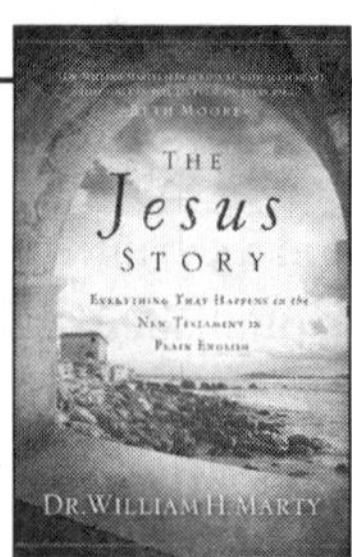

In this book, Dr. William Marty presents the complete narrative of Jesus in an easy-to-read, chronological account. This is a fascinating retelling of everything from his birth to his ascension—as well as what happened in the church after he left. *The Jesus Story* is perfect if you want to get to know Jesus better or recapture the amazement of hearing his story for the first time.

The Jesus Story by Dr. William H. Marty

Reading the Bible can be intimidating, no matter where you are in your faith walk. In this reader-friendly guide to the whole Bible, two respected professors offer helpful book-by-book summaries that cut to the heart of the text, as well as application for what it means to you.

The Quick-Start Guide to the Whole Bible by Dr. William H. Marty and Dr. Boyd Seevers

BETHANYHOUSE

Stay up to date on your favorite books and authors with our free e-newsletters. Sign up today at bethanyhouse.com.

facebook.com/BHPnonfiction

@bethany_house_nonfiction

@bethany_house